Writing Garden

Student book

3

This book belongs to:

How to Use Writing Garden

Writing Prompt

A. Understand the Prompt

Students read and circle the important words. They learn how to understand the question properly and how to prepare for what they will write on their own.

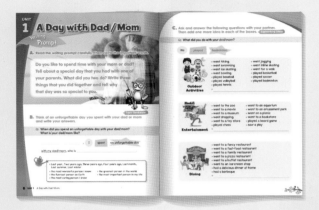

B. Topic Sentence

Students answer the given question for their own topic sentence. Expressions are provided to guide the students.

C. Supporting Ideas

Students ask and answer the questions with their partners. After that, they add one more idea in the blank. This speaking activity will help the students to practice developing relevant supporting ideas, and it will reinforce the acquisition of some of the many different expressions in English. This will also help the students to produce more ideas for their own writing. Expressions are provided to guide the students.

Writing Sprouts

A. Story

Students talk about the pictures and try to guess what the story is about. They learn the key vocabulary with the help of the pictures.

B. Questions with the Graphic Organizer

This comprehension activity will help the students to understand the story better. Students also learn how the ideas are developed and organized with the help of the graphic organizer.

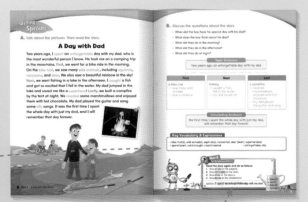

Key Vocabulary & Expressions

Students learn the key vocabulary and expressions.

Hunt for Sentence Parts

Students learn sentence structures by identifying the subject, verb, object, and complement in a sentence.

Writing Process

Planning

Students brainstorm their ideas with the teacher and write them in the blanks. Students are encouraged to write any ideas that come to mind. The activities in *Writing Prompt* can help to guide the students.

Adding Details

Depending on the level of the students, they can either use the examples in the box to answer the questions, or they can write their own answers to the questions. This activity helps the students practice writing a paragraph by incorporating a topic sentence, supporting ideas, and a concluding sentence.

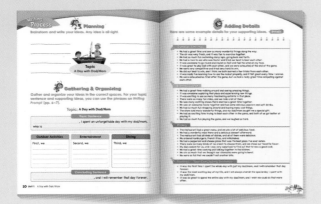

Gathering & Organizing

Students develop and organize their own ideas from the planning stage. The idea organizer will guide the students in writing their ideas in a more organized way.

My 1st Draft

Through the activity of rewriting the story, students can learn how a paragraph is developed, while at the same time reinforcing good writing skills. Students peer-check their writing using the checklist at the bottom of the page. This will help the students to learn correct sentence structure.

Workbook

Expanding Sentences

Students expand the sentences by answering the questions who, what, where, when, and why or how. This activity will help the students learn how to write longer sentences.

Sentence Practice

Students perform exercises in sentence-combining, subject-verb agreement, and various grammar constructs.

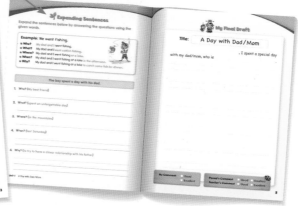

My Final Draft

Students write more sentences and revise their 1st draft. Then students make sure there are no mistakes in their final draft. Students can experience and understand the entire writing process by going through the exercises given in the first step (Planning) to the last step (My Final Draft).

Revising Practice

Students find mistakes in the sentences and correct them. This activity will help the students learn how to revise their writing.

Contents

Unit	Title	Writing Type	Writing Structure	Page
1	A Day with Dad/Mom	Narrative	Personal Narrative Writing	6
2	The Money Tree	Narrative	Personal Narrative Writing	14
3	The Best Vacation Ever	Descriptive	Describing Events	22
4	Three Wishes	Descriptive	Describing Objects	30
Review	Review Units 1 & 2			38
	Review Units 3 & 4			40
5	A Sports Star I Want to Be Like	Expository	Explaining a Role Model	42
6	Places I Want to Visit	Expository	Explaining Desires to Travel	50
7	A Strange/Funny Happening	Expository	Explaining What Happened	58
8	The Best Job in the World	Persuasive	Persuading Through Reasoning	66
Review	Review Units 5 & 6			74
	Review Units 7 & 8			76

Writing Help Pages 78-79   Answer Key Page 80   Activity Cards   Review Stickers

Example: Danny plants flowers.

My hero is my dad.

C (complement)

O (object)

V (verb)

S (subject)

S (subject)
V (verb)
O (object)
C (complement)
Others

Danny plants flowers in his backyard.

S: Who plants flowers? Danny.

V: What does Danny do? He plants flowers.

O: What does Danny plant? He plants flowers.

Others: Where does Danny plant flowers?
He plants flowers in his backyard.

My hero is my dad.

C: Who is your hero? My hero is my dad.

A Day with Dad/Mom

Writing Prompt

A. Read the writing prompt carefully. Then circle the important words.

Do you like to spend time with your mom or dad? Tell about a special day that you had with one of your parents. What did you two do? Write three things that you did together and tell why that day was so special to you.

Topic Sentence

B. Think of an unforgettable day you spent with your dad or mom and write your answers.

Q: When did you spend an unforgettable day with your dad/mom?
What is your dad/mom like?

_____ , I spent an unforgettable day

with my dad/mom, who is _____ .

- Last year, Two years ago, Three years ago, Four years ago, Last month, Last summer, Last winter
- the most wonderful person I know
- the funniest person on Earth
- the most caring person I know
- the greatest person in the world
- the most important person in my life

C. Ask and answer the following questions with your partner. Then add one more idea in each of the boxes. ◄ **Supporting Ideas**

Q: What did you do with your dad/mom?

We ▸ played ▸ badminton.

Outdoor Activities

- went hiking
- went swimming
- went ice skating
- went bowling
- played baseball
- played volleyball
- played tennis
- _____

- went jogging
- went inline skating
- went for a walk
- played basketball
- played soccer
- played badminton

Entertainment

- went to the zoo
- went to a movie
- went to a museum
- went shopping
- went to a toy store
- played chess
- _____

- went to an aquarium
- went to an amusement park
- went on a picnic
- went to a bookstore
- played a board game
- saw a play

Dining

- went to a fancy restaurant
- went to a fast-food restaurant
- went to a family restaurant
- went to a pizza restaurant
- went to a buffet restaurant
- went to an ice-cream shop
- had a delicious dinner at home
- had a barbeque
- _____

A. Talk about the pictures. Then read the story.

A Day with Dad

Two years ago, I spent an unforgettable day with my dad, who is the most wonderful person I know. He took me on a camping trip in the mountains. First, we went for a bike ride in the morning. On the bike trail, we saw many wild animals, including squirrels, raccoons, and deer. We also saw a beautiful rainbow in the sky! Next, we went fishing in a lake in the afternoon. I caught a fish and got so excited that I fell in the water. My dad jumped in the lake and saved me like a superhero! Lastly, we built a campfire by the tent at night. We roasted some marshmallows and enjoyed them with hot chocolate. My dad played the guitar and sang some silly songs. It was the first time I spent the whole day with just my dad, and I will remember that day forever.

B. Discuss the questions about the story.

- When did the boy have his special day with his dad?
- What does the boy think about his dad?
- What did they do in the morning?
- What did they do in the afternoon?
- What did they do at night?

Topic Sentence

two years ago, an unforgettable day with my dad

First

a bike ride
→ saw many wild animals
→ saw a rainbow

Next

fishing
→ caught a fish, fell in the water
→ my dad saved me

Last

a campfire
→ roasted marshmallows, enjoyed with hot chocolate
→ my dad played the guitar and sang

Concluding Sentence

the first time I spent the whole day with just my dad, will remember that day forever

Key Vocabulary & Expressions

- bike trail(s), wild animal(s), squirrel(s), raccoon(s), deer (deer), superhero(es)
- spend/spent, catch/caught, roast/roasted
- unforgettable, silly

Hunt for Sentence Parts

Read the story again and do as follows:

1. Draw circles on the subjects.
2. Draw rectangles on the verbs.
3. Draw stars on the objects.
4. Draw leaves on the complements.

Example I spent an unforgettable day with my dad.

Subject S
Verb V
Object O
Complement C

9

Writing Process

Planning

Brainstorm and write your ideas. Any idea is all right.

_____   _____

_____   _____

_____   _____

_____   _____

Topic
A Day with Dad/Mom

Gathering & Organizing

Gather and organize your ideas in the correct spaces. For your topic sentence and supporting ideas, you can use the phrases on *Writing Prompt* (pp. 6–7).

Topic: A Day with Dad/Mom

Topic Sentence
_____, I spent an unforgettable day with my dad/mom, who is _____.

Outdoor Activities	Entertainment	Dining
First, we _____ _____ _____ _____ .	Second, we _____ _____ _____ _____ .	Third, we _____ _____ _____ _____ .

Concluding Sentence
_____, and I will remember that day forever.

Adding Details

Here are some example details for your supporting ideas. ◀ **Details**

Outdoor Activities

- We had a great time and saw so many wonderful things along the way.
- The air was very fresh, and it was fun to exercise together.
- We had so much fun swimming many laps, going back and forth.
- We had a race to see who was faster and tried our best to beat each other.
- It was awesome to go round and round so fast and feel the wind on my face.
- It was great to play ball with each other, and we were exhausted at the end of the game.
- We were very competitive and tried very hard to win.
- We did our best to win, and I think we both learned a few tricks from each other.
- It was really fun learning how to use the racket properly, and it felt great every time I scored.
- We were exhausted/so tired after the game, but we had a really great time competing against each other.

Entertainment

- We had a great time walking around and seeing amazing things.
- It was awesome exploring that place and experiencing new things.
- It was exciting to see so many fascinating exhibits in that place.
- There were so many fun rides, and we rode a lot of them.
- We saw many exciting shows there and had a great time together.
- We saw an awesome movie together and had some delicious popcorn and soft drinks.
- We had so much fun shopping around and buying many cool things.
- The store sold many wonderful things, and my dad/mom bought me a special gift.
- We had an exciting time trying to beat each other in the game, and both of us got better at playing it.
- We had so much fun playing the game, and we laughed so hard.

Dining

- The restaurant had a great menu, and we ate a lot of delicious food.
- We had a wonderful meal there and a delicious dessert afterward.
- The restaurant had all kinds of dishes, and all of them were delicious.
- We ordered hamburgers, French fries, and milkshakes.
- We had a pepperoni-and-cheese pizza that was the best pizza I've ever eaten.
- There were so many kinds of ice cream to choose from, and we chose our favorite flavor.
- My dad cooked for us, and I was very surprised to find out that he was a good cook.
- We had a great time cooking and talking together in the kitchen.
- We ate so much that we thought our stomachs were going to burst.
- We were so full that we couldn't eat another bite.

Feelings — Your Concluding Sentence

- It was the first time I spent the whole day with just my dad/mom, and I will remember that day forever.
- It was the most exciting day of my life, and I will always cherish the special day I spent with my dad/mom.
- It was so great to spend the entire day with my dad/mom, and I wish we could do that more often.

Answer the questions below. You can write your own answers or choose from the examples on the previous page.

1. **What outdoor activity did you enjoy with your dad/mom?** (Your Supporting Idea 1)

   _____

   What was especially memorable about that outdoor activity? (Details)

   Ⓐ _____

   _____

   Ⓑ _____

   _____

2. **What entertainment did you enjoy with your dad/mom?** (Your Supporting Idea 2)

   _____

   What was especially memorable about that entertainment? (Details)

   Ⓐ _____

   _____

   Ⓑ _____

   _____

3. **What dining experience did you enjoy with your dad/mom?**
   (Your Supporting Idea 3)

   _____

   What was especially memorable about the dining experience? (Details)

   Ⓐ _____

   _____

   Ⓑ _____

   _____

4. **What are your feelings about the special day with your dad/mom?**
   (Your Concluding Sentence)

   _____

   _____

   _____

My 1st Draft

Rewrite your ideas from the previous pages in complete sentences.

Title

A Day with Dad/Mom

Topic Sentence

...., I spent an unforgettable day with my dad/mom, who is ....

Body

....

....

....

....

....

....

....

....

....

....

....

Concluding Sentence

....

....

✔**Peer Proofreading Checklist:**

☐ **Punctuation** ✓capitalization ✓commas(,) ✓periods(.) ✓question marks(?)
☐ **Correct spelling**
☐ **Complete sentences** S + V + end of sentence

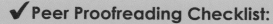

Switch books with your partner and proofread your partner's writing.

➤ After proofreading your 1st draft, rewrite it on your final draft.

Fun Quiz

Q: How many fish did the boy on page 8 catch?

A: He caught _____. <Answer Key p. 80>

The Money Tree

Writing Prompt

A. Read the writing prompt carefully. Then circle the important words.

Imagine that you found a money tree and suddenly became very rich. How would you spend the money from the tree? Tell three things you would do with the money and give reasons for your choices.

Topic Sentence

B. Think of your own ideas for spending the money and write your answer.

Q: What would you do if you found a money tree and became very rich?

If I found a money tree, I would use the money for _____

_____.

- myself, my family, and people in need
- myself, my family, and my friends
- myself, my parents, and my relatives
- myself, my mom and dad, and charity

C. Ask and answer the following questions with your partner. Then add one more idea in each of the boxes. Supporting Ideas

Q: What would you do with all that money?

I would buy all the toys <u>in a toy store</u>.

Myself

- travel around the world
- buy my own airplane and travel around on it
- buy a small island for myself
- buy all the toys in a toy store
- get a cool computer and play lots of games
- get all kinds of pets
- eat at my favorite restaurants every day
- eat all the food I like
- _____

Family

- buy a big house for my family
- get a cool car for my dad
- buy some nice clothes for my mom
- get a nice watch for my uncle
- buy some pretty shoes for my aunt
- buy lots of toys for my brother/sister
- get a cool bike for my cousin
- buy many games for my siblings
- buy new cell phones for all my relatives
- _____

Charity

- donate money to help poor people
- build homes for homeless people
- give money to charity
- use the money for hungry children around the world
- donate money to children in need
- make schools for poor children
- use the money to help people who are elderly and lonely
- give money to an animal shelter
- use the money to buy books for libraries
- build hospitals for people who have no money
- _____

A. Talk about the pictures. Then read the story.

The Money Tree

If I found a money tree, I would use the money for myself, for my family, and for charity. First, I would go on a long trip to many foreign countries. I would go to France to visit the Eiffel Tower and the Louvre Museum. After that, I would go to England to see Buckingham Palace and Tower Bridge. Second, I would buy a big house for my family. It would be a two-story house with twelve bedrooms. The house would also have a big swimming pool and a basketball court in the backyard. Finally, I would donate a lot of money to help children in need. There are so many poor and hungry children in the world, and I want to buy food for them. In addition, I would build schools for them so that they could get an education and have a better future. It would be so rewarding to spend the money from the money tree and make everyone happy, including myself.

B. Discuss the questions about the story.

- If the girl found a money tree, what would she do with the money?
- What would she do first?
- What would she do second?
- What would she do last?

Topic Sentence

if I found a money tree, use the money for myself, my family, and charity

Myself

go on a long trip to foreign countries
→ the Eiffel Tower and the Louvre Museum in France
→ Buckingham Palace and Tower Bridge in England

Family

buy a big house
→ a two-story house with twelve bedrooms
→ a big swimming pool and a basketball court

Charity

donate money to help children in need
→ buy food for them
→ build schools for them

Concluding Sentence

so rewarding to spend the money and make everyone happy, including myself

Key Vocabulary & Expressions

- two-story house, basketball court, backyard, education
- donate/donated, build/built
- foreign, rewarding, including
- in addition

Hunt for Sentence Parts

Read the story again and do as follows:

1. Draw circles on the subjects.
2. Draw rectangles on the verbs.
3. Draw stars on the objects.
4. Draw leaves on the complements.

Example I would use the money for myself, for my family, and for charity.

Subject Ⓢ
Verb Ⓥ
Object Ⓞ
Complement Ⓒ

Writing Process

 **Planning**

Brainstorm and write your ideas. Any idea is all right.

_____   _____

_____   _____

_____   _____

Topic
The Money Tree

 Gathering & Organizing

Gather and organize your ideas in the correct spaces. For your topic sentence and supporting ideas, you can use the phrases on *Writing Prompt* (pp. 14–15).

Topic: The Money Tree

Topic Sentence
If I found a money tree, I would use the money for _____ _____.

Myself	Family	Charity
I would _____ _____ _____ _____.	I would _____ _____ _____ _____.	I would _____ _____ _____ _____.

Concluding Sentence
It would be _____.

Adding Details

Myself

- There are so many places that I want to see, and I would visit all of them.
- It would be so great to travel and see the world.
- My private airplane would take me anywhere I want to go.
- I would relax on the beach and swim every day.
- I would have a great time playing with the toys, and I would never be bored.
- It would be so exciting to play games on my own computer.
- There are so many pets that I want to have, and I would buy all of them.
- I would eat three delicious meals each day.
- Tasty food makes me happy, and I would eat my favorite foods at every meal.
- I would eat the best foods in the most expensive restaurants.
- I love going to fancy restaurants, so I would eat at a fancy restaurant every day.
- I would eat lobster and steak whenever I want.

Family

- The house would have twenty bedrooms and six bathrooms.
- The house would also have a big swimming pool with a cool slide.
- The house would also have a large family room.
- The car would look very fancy and rich.
- The car would be a sports car and go very fast.
- It/They would make him/her/them very happy, and he/she/they would look nice with it/them.
- It/They would make him/her/them very excited, and he/she/they would enjoy it/them very much.
- It/They would be the latest model.

Charity

- There are many people who need help desperately, and I want to help them.
- There are so many people without homes, and I want to build homeless shelters for them.
- Many children are starving, and I want to help feed them.
- Many children don't have parents, so I would support them with my money.
- I would spend some of the money to help kids go to college/get an education.
- I would use the money to do things for the elderly people who are lonely.
- The money would be used to build social centers for elderly people so they would not be lonely.
- The money would be used to help abandoned or abused animals.
- The books would help people learn lots of important things.
- They would provide medical care for poor people.

Feelings – Your Concluding Sentence

- It would be so great if I found a money tree and spent the money on these three special things.
- It would be so wonderful to find a money tree and spend the money on things that would make me and others happy.

Answer the questions below. You can write your own answers or choose from the examples on the previous page.

1. **How would you spend the money on yourself?** (Your Supporting Idea 1)

   _____

   Add two more sentences for your choice. (Details)

   A _____

   _____

   B _____

   _____

2. **How would you spend the money on your family?** (Your Supporting Idea 2)

   _____

   Add two more sentences for your choice. (Details)

   A _____

   _____

   B _____

   _____

3. **How would you use the money for charity?** (Your Supporting Idea 3)

   _____

   Add two more sentences for your choice. (Details)

   A _____

   _____

   B _____

   _____

4. **What are your feelings about spending the money from the money tree like that?**
   (Your Concluding Sentence)

   _____

   _____

   _____

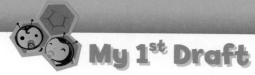

My 1st Draft

Rewrite your ideas from the previous pages in complete sentences.

Title

The Money Tree

Topic Sentence

If I found a money tree, I would use the money for

Body

Concluding Sentence

✓**Peer Proofreading Checklist:**

☐ **Punctuation** ✓capitalization ✓commas(,) ✓periods(.) ✓question marks(?)
☐ **Correct spelling**
☐ **Complete sentences** S + V + end of sentence

Switch books with your partner and proofread your partner's writing.

↳ After proofreading your 1st draft, rewrite it on your final draft.

Fun Quiz

Q: In the picture at the top of page 16, what is the girl under the tree doing?
A: She _____. <Answer Key p. 80>

Writing Prompt

A. Read the writing prompt carefully. Then circle the important words.

When was the best vacation you have ever had? Where did you go? What did you see and do? Write about that vacation and give three reasons why it was the best one ever.

Topic Sentence

B. Think of your own best vacation and write your answers.

Q: When was the best vacation you have ever had? Where did you go? Who were you with? And how long was it?

_____, I **went** to _____

with my _____ for _____, and

it **was** the best vacation I have ever had.

- Last summer, Last winter, Last year, Two years ago, Six months ago
- the mountains, the beach, a lake, an island, a ski resort
- family, friends, grandparents, relatives, classmates
- a day, two days, three days, four days, five days, a week, a month

C. Ask and answer the following questions with your partner. Then add one more idea in each of the boxes. ◄ **Supporting Ideas**

Q: What did you see and do during your vacation?

We   saw   a lot of interesting places and   did   so many fun things.

Activities

- There were so many exciting activities to do.
- There were a lot of activities we could enjoy.
- We did so many fun activities there.
- The place had many interesting activities to do.
- The place offered all kinds of exciting activities.
- We enjoyed doing many exciting activities.
- _____

Sights

- We enjoyed the spectacular scenery.
- We got to see some breathtaking views.
- We couldn't get over the amazing landscape.
- We experienced some beautiful scenery.
- We were moved by the beauty of nature.
- We were thrilled by the fantastic landscape.
- We were filled with wonder at the beauty of nature.
- _____

Experience

- It was a great chance to spend time with my family.
- We really enjoyed our time together.
- We had a great time during the trip.
- We became much closer during the trip.
- We came to know each other much better.
- We had a fantastic time together.
- We had so much fun together.
- We were happy to share each other's company.
- The trip really brought us closer together.
- _____

A. Talk about the pictures. Then read the story.

The Best Vacation Ever

Last summer, I spent three days with my family in the Grand Canyon, and it was the best vacation I've ever had. First of all, there were so many great activities we could enjoy in the Grand Canyon. My family hiked down a steep trail and went to the bottom of the canyon. We also rode a raft and paddled down the Colorado River. Secondly, the scenery of the Grand Canyon was wonderful. From the viewpoints, we could see the fantastic views of the rocky canyon walls and the colorful landscape. We even watched a beautiful sunset in the evening. Lastly, it was a great chance to spend time with each other. We talked and laughed so much during the trip. Spending three days together made us realize that family is the most important thing in the world. The family vacation to the Grand Canyon will always have a special place in my heart, and I hope we can have many more wonderful family vacations like that in the future.

B. Discuss the questions about the story.

- Where did the boy go with his family on vacation?
- What activities did the family enjoy?
- What sights did they see?
- What did they realize from their vacation together?

Topic Sentence

last summer, I spent three days with my family in the Grand Canyon

Activities

so many activities to enjoy
→ hiked down a steep trail to the bottom of the canyon
→ rode a raft and paddled down the Colorado River

Sights

the scenery was wonderful
→ could see the fantastic views of the canyon walls and the colorful landscape
→ watched a beautiful sunset in the evening

Experience

a great chance to spend time with each other
→ talked and laughed so much
→ made us realize that family is the most important thing in the world

Concluding Sentence

the family vacation will have a special place in my heart, I hope we can have many more family vacations like that

Key Vocabulary & Expressions

- activity (activities), raft(s), scenery, viewpoint(s), view(s), landscape(s), sunset(s)
- spend/spent, hike/hiked, paddle/paddled, realize/realized
- steep, fantastic   • during

Hunt for Sentence Parts

Read the story again and do as follows:
1. Draw circles on the subjects.
2. Draw rectangles on the verbs.
3. Draw stars on the objects.
4. Draw leaves on the complements.

Example I spent three days with my family in the Grand Canyon.

Subject Ⓢ
Verb Ⓥ
Object Ⓞ
Complement Ⓒ

25

Writing Process

Planning

Brainstorm and write your ideas. Any idea is all right.

_____

_____

_____

_____

_____

_____

Topic
The Best Vacation Ever

Gathering & Organizing

Gather and organize your ideas in the correct spaces. For your topic sentence and supporting ideas, you can use the phrases on *Writing Prompt* (pp. 22–23).

Topic: The Best Vacation Ever

> ### Topic Sentence
> _____, I went to _____ with my _____ for _____, and it was the best vacation I've ever had.

Activities	Sights	Experience
_____	_____	_____
_____	_____	_____
_____	_____	_____
_____ .	_____ .	_____ .

> ### Concluding Sentence
> The vacation to _____ will always have a special place in my heart, and I _____.

Adding Details

Here are some example details for your supporting ideas. **Details**

Activities

- We went hiking to the top of the mountain.
- We went camping in the mountains.
- We made many sandcastles on the beach.
- We enjoyed swimming in the ocean.
- We went fishing in the lake.
- We swam in the lake.
- We had a tour of the island.
- We rode bikes around the island.
- We skied on some really soft snow.
- We skied on some really exciting slopes.

Sights

- The mountains and the trees were just amazing.
- The sky was so clear and blue.
- We saw a bright orange sky at sunset.
- We watched the sunrise early in the morning.
- We saw so many stars in the night sky.
- We saw a rainbow high in the sky.
- The water was so clear and blue.
- We saw snow-covered mountains for the first time.
- We were really moved by the power and the beauty of nature.
- We saw beautiful eagles flying high above the lake.

Experience

- We talked so much about everything.
- It was a great chance for us to find out how important we are to each other.
- We realized that family is the most important thing in the world.
- Time went by really quickly because we were having so much fun.
- We were laughing the whole time we were on vacation.
- I got to know my mother/father/brother/sister better.
- I learned a lot about myself and my abilities.
- We had a great time together enjoying the wonders of nature.
- We had such a great time that the vacation was over before we knew it.
- The experience was physically exhausting, but I think it made me a better person.

Feelings — Your Concluding Sentence

- I hope we can do this again in the near future.
- I can't wait to go on another vacation with the people I love.
- I look forward to many more vacations like this in the future.

Answer the questions below. You can write your own answers or choose from the examples on the previous page.

1. **What activities did you enjoy during your vacation?** (Your Supporting Idea 1)

   _____

   Write two more sentences about the activities you enjoyed. (Details)

   A _____

   _____

   B _____

   _____

2. **What did you think about the scenery during your vacation?**
   (Your Supporting Idea 2)

   _____

   Write two more sentences about the scenery you saw. (Details)

   A _____

   _____

   B _____

   _____

3. **What did you experience personally during the trip?** (Your Supporting Idea 3)

   _____

   Write two more sentences about how the vacation affected you personally. (Details)

   A _____

   _____

   B _____

   _____

4. **What are your feelings about your best vacation ever?**
   (Your Concluding Sentence)

   _____

   _____

   _____

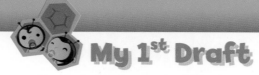 My 1st Draft

Rewrite your ideas from the previous pages in complete sentences.

Title

The Best Vacation Ever

Topic Sentence

_____, I went to _____
with my _____ for _____, and
it was the best vacation I've ever had.

Body

_____

_____

_____

_____

_____

_____

_____

_____

_____

Concluding Sentence

_____

_____

✔ Peer Proofreading Checklist:

☐ **Punctuation** ✔capitalization ✔commas(,) ✔periods(.) ✔question marks(?)
☐ **Correct spelling**
☐ **Complete sentences** S + V + end of sentence

Switch books with your partner and proofread your partner's writing.

→ After proofreading your 1st draft, rewrite it on your final draft.

Fun Quiz

Q: On page 24, how many people are paddling the raft?

A: There are _____. <Answer Key p. 80>

Three Wishes

Writing Prompt

A. Read the writing prompt carefully. Then circle the important words.

Suppose you found a magic lamp. You rubbed the lamp and a genie came out and offered to grant you three wishes. What would you wish for? Why would you choose those wishes? Give reasons for your choices.

> Topic Sentence

B. Think of your own three wishes and write your answer.

Q: If you found a magic lamp and a genie granted you three wishes, how would it make you feel?

If I found a magic lamp and a genie granted me three wishes,

it   would make   ⭐   me   feel _____.

- very happy
- overjoyed
- delighted

- very excited
- thrilled

C. Ask and answer the following questions with your partner. Then add one more idea in each of the boxes. **Supporting Ideas**

Q: What would you ask for?

I would ask for a homework robot.

- a homework robot
- an entertainment robot
- a tooth-brushing robot
- a hair-styling robot
- _____

- a robot teacher
- a shower robot
- a bed-making robot
- a good-friend robot

Wish 1

- a pair of flying shoes
- a self-driving car
- a flying bicycle
- a time machine
- _____

- a flying hat
- a flying car
- a teleporter

Wish 2

- a cleaning robot
- a cooking machine
- a security robot
- a dog-washing machine
- _____

- a cooking robot
- a window-washing robot
- a candy machine

Wish 3

Writing Sprouts

A. Talk about the pictures. Then read the story.

Three Wishes

If I found a magic lamp and a genie granted me three wishes, it would make me feel very happy. The first thing I would ask for is a homework machine. It would look like a pizza box that I could put my textbook in. The homework machine would do my homework for me so that I could have more time to play. The second thing I would ask for is a flying car. It would look like a sports car with short wings. The flying car would take me anywhere I want to go so that I could visit many famous places in the world. The third thing I would ask for is a cleaning robot for my mom. It would look like an octopus with many arms. The cleaning robot would do house cleaning for my mom so that she would have more time to relax. If my wishes could come true, it would make our lives very convenient and comfortable.

B. Discuss the questions about the story.

- If the boy found a magic lamp and a genie granted him three wishes, how would it make him feel?

- What is the first thing the boy would ask for? Why?

- What is the second thing the boy would ask for? Why?

- What is the third thing the boy would ask for? Why?

Topic Sentence

if I found a magic lamp and a genie granted me three wishes, make me feel very happy

Wish 1	Wish 2	Wish 3
a homework machine would → look like a pizza box → do my homework	a flying car would → look like a sports car with short wings → take me anywhere I want to go	a cleaning robot for mom would → look like an octopus → do house cleaning

Concluding Sentence

if my wishes could come true, make our lives convenient and comfortable

Key Vocabulary & Expressions

- magic lamp(s), genie(s), machine(s), textbook(s), wing(s)
- grant/granted, visit/visited, relax/relaxed
- famous, convenient, comfortable

Hunt for Sentence Parts

Read the story again and do as follows:
1. Draw circles on the subjects.
2. Draw rectangles on the verbs.
3. Draw stars on the objects.
4. Draw leaves on the complements.

Example It would make me feel very happy.

Subject Ⓢ
Verb Ⓥ
Object Ⓞ
Complement Ⓒ

 **Planning**

Brainstorm and write your ideas. Any idea is all right.

_____   _____

_____   _____

_____   _____

_____   _____

Topic
Three Wishes

Gathering & Organizing

Gather and organize your ideas in the correct spaces. For your topic sentence and supporting ideas, you can use the phrases on *Writing Prompt* (pp. 30–31).

Topic: Three Wishes

Topic Sentence
If I found a magic lamp and a genie granted me three wishes, it would make me feel _____.

Wish 1	Wish 2	Wish 3
The first thing I would ask for is _____ _____ _____ _____.	The second thing I would ask for is _____ _____ _____ _____.	The third thing I would ask for is _____ _____ _____ _____.

Concluding Sentence
If my wishes could come true, it would make my life _____.

Adding Details

Here are some example details for your supporting ideas. **Details**

Wish 1

- It would look like a human, talk like a human, and act like a human.
- It would look like a real human being, and I could talk to it.
- The homework robot would help me do my homework so that I could play more.
- The robot teacher would teach me many things so that I would become a genius.
- The entertainment robot would sing and dance for me when I am sad and lonely to cheer me up.
- The shower robot would give me a shower so that I could keep myself nice and clean.
- The tooth-brushing robot would brush my teeth so that my teeth would always be bright and white.
- The bed-making robot would make my bed so that my bedroom would always look tidy and clean.
- The hair-styling robot would take care of my hair so that it would always look stylish.
- The good-friend robot would play with me all the time so that I would never be lonely.

Wish 2

- The flying shoes would look like a pair of basketball shoes with tiny wings on them.
- The flying shoes would have wings that would make me fly like a bird.
- The flying hat would look like a safety helmet with a small propeller on top.
- The flying hat would have propellers and take me high up into the air.
- The self-driving car would look like a sports car with a computer instead of an engine.
- The flying car would look like a racing car with huge wings.
- The flying bicycle would look like a mountain bicycle with wing-shaped pedals.
- The teleporter would look like a big box with many buttons.
- It/They would take me to school so that I would always get there on time.
- It/They would take me anywhere I want to go so that I wouldn't have to walk anywhere.
- It/They would let me travel from one place to another quickly so that I could save a lot of time.
- It/They would allow me to travel into the past or the future so that I could experience interesting things.

Wish 3

- The cleaning robot would look like a spider with eight legs.
- The cooking robot would look like a cook with an apron and a hat.
- The cooking machine would look like a microwave oven with many buttons.
- The window-washing robot would look like a person with many arms.
- The window-washing robot would look like a human being with long arms.
- The security robot would look like a real policeman in a uniform.
- The cleaning robot would clean my house so that it would be spotless.
- The cooking robot would cook for me so that I could eat delicious food at every meal.
- The cooking machine would make any food I want so that I could enjoy lots of delicious meals.
- The window-washing robot would wash all the windows of my house so that they would look clean and shiny.
- The security robot would guard my house so that my family could be safe all the time.

Feelings — Your Concluding Sentence

- If my wishes could come true, it would make my life very fun and convenient.
- If my wishes could come true, it would make my life very exciting and comfortable.
- If my wishes could come true, it would make my life very convenient and enjoyable.

Answer the questions below. You can write your own answers or choose from the examples on the previous page.

1. **What would you ask for with your first wish?** (Your Supporting Idea 1)

   _____

   What would the thing you wished for look like? What would it do? (Details)

   Ⓐ _____

   _____

   Ⓑ _____

   _____

2. **What would you ask for with your second wish?** (Your Supporting Idea 2)

   _____

   What would the thing you wished for look like? What would it do? (Details)

   Ⓐ _____

   _____

   Ⓑ _____

   _____

3. **What would you ask for with your third wish?** (Your Supporting Idea 3)

   _____

   What would the thing you wished for look like? What would it do? (Details)

   Ⓐ _____

   _____

   Ⓑ _____

   _____

4. **What are your feelings about the three wishes coming true?**

   (Your Concluding Sentence)

   _____

   _____

   _____

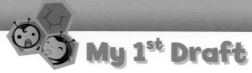

My 1st Draft

Rewrite your ideas from the previous pages in complete sentences.

Title

Three Wishes

Topic Sentence

If I found a magic lamp and a genie granted me three wishes, it would make me feel _____ .

Body

Concluding Sentence

✔ **Peer Proofreading Checklist:**

- [ ] **Punctuation** ✔capitalization ✔commas(,) ✔periods(.) ✔question marks(?)
- [ ] **Correct spelling**
- [ ] **Complete sentences** S + V + end of sentence

Switch books with your partner and proofread your partner's writing.

➤ After proofreading your 1st draft, rewrite it on your final draft.

Fun Quiz

Q: In the picture on page 32, how many legs does the cleaning robot have?

A: It _____ . <Answer Key p. 80>

A. Write the past tense.

1. spend _____
2. go _____
3. take _____
4. see _____
5. catch _____

6. find _____
7. buy _____
8. build _____
9. get _____
10. donate _____

B. Complete the topic and concluding sentences using the phrases from the box below.

1. If I found a money tree, I would use the money for _____

   _____.

2. It was the first time I spent the whole day with just my dad, _____

   _____.

3. It would be so rewarding to spend the money from the money tree and _____

   _____.

4. Two years ago, I spent an unforgettable day with my dad, who _____

   _____.

- make everyone happy, including myself
- and I will remember that day forever
- myself, for my family, and for charity
- is the most wonderful person I know

C. Write the proper supporting ideas from the box below.

1. _____

   I caught a fish and got so excited that I fell in the water. My dad jumped in the lake and saved me like a superhero!

2. _____

   There are so many poor and hungry children in the world, and I want to buy food for them. In addition, I would build schools for them so that they could get an education and have a better future.

3. _____

   We roasted some marshmallows and enjoyed them with hot chocolate. My dad played the guitar and sang some silly songs.

4. _____

   It would be a two-story house with twelve bedrooms. The house would also have a big swimming pool and a basketball court in the backyard.

5. _____

   I would go to France to visit the Eiffel Tower and the Louvre Museum. After that, I would go to England to see Buckingham Palace and Tower Bridge.

6. _____

   On the bike trail, we saw many wild animals, including squirrels, raccoons, and deer. We also saw a beautiful rainbow in the sky!

- Lastly, we built a campfire by the tent at night.
- Next, we went fishing in a lake in the afternoon.
- Finally, I would donate a lot of money to help children in need.
- First, we went for a bike ride in the morning.
- Second, I would buy a big house for my family.
- First, I would go on a long trip to many foreign countries.

sticker

 Activity cards are available at the back of the book.

Review Units 3 & 4

A. Write the past tense.

1. is _____ are _____
2. can _____
3. hike _____
4. paddle _____
5. realize _____

6. make _____
7. grant _____
8. ask _____
9. come _____
10. relax _____

B. Complete the topic and concluding sentences using the phrases from the box below.

1. If I found a magic lamp and a genie granted me three wishes, it _____

    _____.

2. The family vacation to the Grand Canyon will always have a special place in

    my heart, and I hope we can _____

    _____.

3. Last summer, I spent three days with my family in the Grand Canyon, and it

    was _____.

4. If my wishes could come true, _____

    _____.

- it would make our lives very convenient and comfortable
- the best vacation I've ever had
- have many more wonderful family vacations like that in the future
- would make me feel very happy

C. Write the proper supporting ideas from the box below.

1. _____

It would look like an octopus with many arms. The cleaning robot would do house cleaning for my mom so that she would have more time to relax.

2. _____

It would look like a pizza box that I could put my textbook in. The homework machine would do my homework for me so that I could have more time to play.

3. _____

From the viewpoints, we could see the fantastic views of the rocky canyon walls and the colorful landscape. We even watched a beautiful sunset in the evening.

4. _____

We talked and laughed so much during the trip. Spending three days together made us realize that family is the most important thing in the world.

5. _____

My family hiked down a steep trail and went to the bottom of the canyon. We also rode a raft and paddled down the Colorado River.

6. _____

It would look like a sports car with short wings. The flying car would take me anywhere I want to go so that I could visit many famous places in the world.

- The third thing I would ask for is a cleaning robot for my mom.
- The first thing I would ask for is a homework machine.
- The second thing I would ask for is a flying car.
- Secondly, the scenery of the Grand Canyon was wonderful.
- Lastly, it was a great chance to spend time with each other.
- First of all, there were so many great activities we could enjoy in the Grand Canyon.

 Activity cards are available at the back of the book.

A Sports Star I Want to Be Like

Writing Prompt

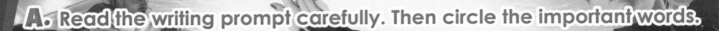

A. Read the writing prompt carefully. Then circle the important words.

Have you ever dreamed of being a sports star? What is your favorite sport? Who is your favorite sports star? Why do you want to be like that sports star?

Topic Sentence

B. Think of your own favorite sport and favorite sports star and write your answers.

Q: What is your favorite sport? Which favorite sports star do you want to be like?

_____ is my favorite sport, and I want to be

like (a sports star of your choice) _____, who is

_____.

- Soccer, Baseball, Basketball, Football, Volleyball, Tennis, Speed skating, Figure skating, Swimming, Golf
- a soccer player, a baseball player, a basketball player, a football player, a volleyball player, a tennis player, a speed skater, a figure skater, a swimmer, a golfer

C. Ask and answer the following questions with your partner. Then add one more idea in each of the boxes. Supporting Ideas

Q: Why do you want to be like the sports star?

I · want · to be · like him/her · because he/she **is the greatest athlete**

in the world.

Skills

- is the greatest athlete in the world
- is the best soccer/baseball/basketball/football/ volleyball/tennis player ever
- is the greatest sportsman/sportswoman of all time
- is an unbeatable player
- is the best player to ever play the game of soccer/ baseball/basketball/tennis
- _____

Riches & Fame

- is very rich and famous
- makes a lot of money, and everybody knows him/her
- is a millionaire and very famous
- earns so much money, and everyone knows who he/she is
- is the highest-paid and best-known athlete in the world
- _____

Personality

- is a warm-hearted person
- is generous
- is a giving person
- is a charitable person
- is a very kind person
- loves his/her fans
- _____

A. Talk about the pictures. Then read the story.

A Sports Star I Want to Be Like

Figure skating is my favorite sport, and I want to be like Kim Yuna, who is a South Korean figure skater. The first reason that I want to be like Kim Yuna is because she is one of the greatest female figure skaters in the world. Her skating is so beautiful, graceful, and powerful. Also, she has won many medals, including a gold medal at the 2010 Winter Olympic Games. The second reason that I want to be like Kim Yuna is because she is very rich and famous. She earns a lot of money from competitions and advertising. Moreover, she is so famous that fans follow her everywhere. The last reason that I want to be like Kim Yuna is because she has a warm and generous heart. She donates a lot of money to charity. In addition, she is a UNICEF Goodwill Ambassador and helps people in need around the world. It would be wonderful if I grew up to be like Kim Yuna, who is almost perfect in every way.

B. Discuss the questions about the story.

- What is the girl's favorite sport?
- Which favorite sports star does the girl want to be like?
- What is the first reason that she wants to be like the sports star?
- What is the second reason that she wants to be like the sports star?
- What is the last reason that she wants to be like the sports star?

Topic Sentence

figure skating is my favorite sport, want to be like Kim Yuna, a South Korean figure skater

Skills

one of the greatest female figure skaters in the world
→ her skating is beautiful, graceful, and powerful
→ won many medals

Riches & Fame

rich and famous
→ earns a lot of money from competitions and advertising
→ fans follow her everywhere

Personality

has a warm and generous heart
→ donates money to charity
→ a UNICEF Goodwill Ambassador

Concluding Sentence

would be wonderful if I grew up to be like Kim Yuna

Key Vocabulary & Expressions

- figure skating, medal(s), competition(s), advertising, fan(s), charity (charities), UNICEF Goodwill Ambassador(s)
- earn/earned, donate/donated
- female, graceful, powerful, generous, perfect
- moreover

Hunt for Sentence Parts

Read the story again and do as follows:
1. Draw circles on the subjects.
2. Draw rectangles on the verbs.
3. Draw stars on the objects.
4. Draw leaves on the complements.

Example **Figure skating** is my favorite sport.

Subject Ⓢ
Verb Ⓥ
Object Ⓞ
Complement Ⓒ

Planning

Brainstorm and write your ideas. Any idea is all right.

_____   _____

_____   _____

_____   **Topic**   _____
                      A Sports Star
_____   I Want to Be Like

Gathering & Organizing

Gather and organize your ideas in the correct spaces. For your topic sentence and supporting ideas, you can use the phrases on *Writing Prompt* (pp. 42–43).

Topic: A Sports Star I Want to Be Like

Topic Sentence
_____ is my favorite sport, and I want to be like _____ , who is _____ .

Skills	Riches & Fame	Personality
He/She _____	He/She _____	He/She _____
_____	_____	_____
_____	_____	_____
_____	_____	_____
_____ .	_____ .	_____ .

Concluding Sentence
It would be wonderful if _____ .

Adding Details

Here are some example details for your supporting ideas. **Details**

Skills

- He/She can play the sport very well.
- He/She is a very skillful player.
- He/She practices many hours a day to be the best.
- He/She is a powerful and outstanding player.
- He/She is the strongest player in the game.
- He/She is super competitive and does whatever he/she can to win.
- He/She is very competitive and never gives up.
- He/She is the fastest man/woman alive.
- He/She has won many sports awards/medals/trophies.
- He/She can do things with a soccer ball/basketball that no other person can do.

Riches & Fame

- He/She gets a lot of money from competitions.
- He/She makes a lot of money from playing the sport.
- He/She earns lots of money from advertising.
- He/She gets so much money from competitions and advertising.
- He/She has many fans that love him/her.
- He/She is the best-loved athlete in the sport.
- He/She is always signing autographs for his/her fans.
- He/She is so famous that everybody wants his/her autograph.
- He/She is so great that everyone knows who he/she is.
- He/She is recognized everywhere he/she goes.

Personality

- He/She is very humble and sincere.
- He/She doesn't put himself/herself above other people.
- He/She doesn't let his/her fame go to his/her head.
- He/She donates a large sum of money to charity.
- He/She does a lot of charity work.
- He/She does a lot of volunteer work for needy people.
- He/She works with disadvantaged children to teach them the sport.
- He/She works hard to help protect the environment.
- He/She works very hard to help save endangered animals.
- He/She helps abused or abandoned animals.
- He/She gives scholarships to children in need.

Feelings — Your Concluding Sentence

- It would be wonderful if I grew up to be like my favorite sports star, who is almost perfect in every way.
- I wish I could grow up to be like my favorite sports star, who is my idol.
- I want to grow up to be like my favorite sports star, who is my role model.

Answer the questions below. You can write your own answers or choose from the examples on the previous page.

1. **What skills does your favorite sports star have?** (Your Supporting Idea 1)

   _____

   Give two examples. (Details)

   (A) _____

   _____

   (B) _____

   _____

2. **How rich and famous is your favorite sports star?** (Your Supporting Idea 2)

   _____

   Give two examples. (Details)

   (A) _____

   _____

   (B) _____

   _____

3. **What kind of personality does your favorite sports star have?**
   (Your Supporting Idea 3)

   _____

   Give two examples. (Details)

   (A) _____

   _____

   (B) _____

   _____

4. **What are your feelings about your favorite sports star?**
   (Your Concluding Sentence)

   _____

   _____

   _____

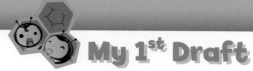 **My 1ˢᵗ Draft**

Rewrite your ideas from the previous pages in complete sentences.

Title

> ## A Sports Star I Want to Be Like

Topic Sentence

_____ is my favorite sport, and I want to
be like _____, who is _____.

Body

_____

_____

_____

_____

_____

_____

_____

_____

_____

_____

Concluding Sentence

_____

_____

✔ **Peer Proofreading Checklist:**

☐ **Punctuation** ✔capitalization ✔commas(,) ✔periods(.) ✔question marks(?)
☐ **Correct spelling**
☐ **Complete sentences** S + V + end of sentence

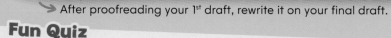 Switch books with your partner and proofread your partner's writing.

➤ After proofreading your 1ˢᵗ draft, rewrite it on your final draft.

Fun Quiz

Q: On page 44, what does the girl in the blue shirt have around her neck?
A: It _____. <Answer Key p. 80>

Writing Prompt

A. Read the writing prompt carefully. Then circle the important words.

If you could go anywhere in the world, where would you go? What are three places you would like to visit? Why do you want to go there? What would you see and do there?

Topic Sentence

B. Think of the places that you want to visit and write your answers.

Q: What places in the world do you want to see? What are your plans about these places?

There **are** many _____ places in the world that

I want to see, and someday _____.

- famous, well-known, popular, important, interesting, amazing
- I hope to visit a few of them   • I will visit all of them
- I hope to visit some of them   • I'm going to travel and see as many as I can

C. Ask and answer the following questions with your partner. Then add one more idea in each of the boxes. < Supporting Ideas

Q: What place do you want to visit?

I   want   to visit India.

Asia & Australia

- Korea
- Japan
- China
- India
- Cambodia
- Australia
- _____

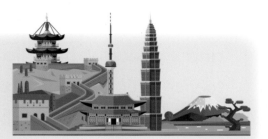

Europe & Africa

- France
- England
- Italy
- Egypt
- _____

The Americas & Antarctica

- the United States of America
- Canada
- Mexico
- Peru
- Antarctica
- _____

A. Talk about the pictures. Then read the story.

Places I Want to Visit

There are many famous places in the world that I want to see, and someday I hope to visit a few of them. One place that I want to visit is Egypt. I am fascinated by the Great Sphinx of Giza, which is a large stone lion with a man's head. Seeing the Great Sphinx of Giza in Egypt would be a dream come true. Another place I want to go to is China. The Great Wall of China is more than 2,300 years old, and it is the longest man-made structure in the world. It would be very exciting to walk along the top of the Great Wall of China. The last place I want to travel to is Italy. The Tower of Pisa there is famous because it is leaning to one side at an angle of about four degrees. I want to go to the Tower of Pisa and actually measure it for myself. I can't wait to visit these places someday and experience the wonders of them all.

B. Discuss the questions about the story.

- What does the boy want to do about the places in the world that he wants to see?
- What does he want to see in Egypt?
- What does he want to see in China?
- What does he want to see in Italy?

Topic Sentence

many places in the world I want to see, hope to visit a few of them

Egypt

the Great Sphinx of Giza
→ a large stone lion with a man's head
→ a dream come true

China

the Great Wall of China
→ more than 2,300 years old, the longest man-made structure
→ exciting to walk along the top of the wall

Italy

the Tower of Pisa
→ leaning to one side at an angle of about four degrees
→ want to go and measure

Concluding Sentence

can't wait to visit these places and experience the wonders of them all

Key Vocabulary & Expressions

- structure(s), angle(s), degree(s), wonder(s)
- lean/leaned, measure/measured, experience/experienced
- fascinated, man-made
- someday, actually

Hunt
for Sentence Parts

Read the story again and do as follows:
1. Draw circles on the subjects.
2. Draw rectangles on the verbs.
3. Draw stars on the objects.
4. Draw leaves on the complements.

Example There are many famous places in the world that I want to see.

Subject Ⓢ
Verb Ⓥ
Object Ⓞ
Complement Ⓒ

Planning

Brainstorm and write your ideas. Any idea is all right.

Topic
Places I Want to Visit

Gathering & Organizing

Gather and organize your ideas in the correct spaces. For your topic sentence and supporting ideas, you can use the phrases on *Writing Prompt* (pp. 50–51).

Topic: Places I Want to Visit

Topic Sentence

There are many _____ places in the world that I want to see, and someday _____.

Asia & Australia	Europe & Africa	The Americas & Antarctica
I want to visit _____ _____ _____ _____ _____ .	I want to visit _____ _____ _____ _____ _____ .	I want to visit _____ _____ _____ _____ _____ .

Concluding Sentence

_____ these places someday.

Adding Details

Here are some example details for your supporting ideas. ‹ **Details**

Asia & Australia

- Gyeongbok Palace in Korea was the first royal palace built during the Joseon Dynasty.
- Mount Fuji in Japan is the highest mountain in Japan, and it is 3,776 meters tall.
- The Forbidden City in China is the largest ancient palace in the world.
- The Taj Mahal is a famous mausoleum in India, built by Emperor Shah Jahan in memory of his wife, Mumtaz Mahal.
- Angkor Wat is a temple complex in Cambodia and is the largest religious monument in the world.
- Sydney Opera House in Australia is one of the most famous performing arts centers in the world.
- Seeing this place would truly be a dream come true.
- It would be really fun and exciting to see it in person.
- It would be like heaven to actually be in the palace.
- It would be the best thing to ever happen to me if I could go there.

Europe & Africa

- The Eiffel Tower is a famous landmark in Paris, France.
- Buckingham Palace in London, England, is the home of the English royal family.
- The Colosseum in Rome, Italy, is an amphitheater built during the time of the Roman Empire.
- The Great Pyramid of Giza was built as a tomb for the Egyptian pharaoh Khufu.
- I want to go there and see how big it really is.
- It would be really exciting to take a photo in front of this famous place.
- It would be really cool to stand where kings have stood.
- It would be really neat to get my picture taken inside the palace.
- It would be great to visit this place because of its long history.

The Americas & Antarctica

- The Statue of Liberty is located in the US, on Liberty Island in New York Harbor.
- Niagara Falls is the second largest waterfall in the world and is located on the border of Ontario, Canada, and New York, USA.
- Chichen Itza is an ancient city built by the Maya people in Mexico.
- Machu Picchu was a city of the Inca Empire and is located 8,000 feet above sea level atop a mountain in the Andes Mountain Range in Peru.
- The Amundsen-Scott South Pole Station in Antarctica is located at the South Pole.
- It would be amazing to actually see it with my own eyes.
- I want to take many pictures of this place.
- It would be the trip of a lifetime to go there.
- It would make me the happiest kid in the world to see it.
- It would be the best experience ever if I could visit it.

Feelings — Your Concluding Sentence

- I can't wait to visit these places of wonder and beauty someday.
- I look forward to visiting these places someday.
- It would be a dream come true to visit all of these places someday.

Answer the questions below. You can write your own answers or choose from the examples on the previous page.

1. **What place in Asia or Australia do you want to visit?** (Your Supporting Idea 1)

    _____

    What would you see and do there? (Details)

    Ⓐ _____

    _____

    Ⓑ _____

    _____

2. **What place in Europe or Africa do you want to visit?** (Your Supporting Idea 2)

    _____

    What would you see and do there? (Details)

    Ⓐ _____

    _____

    Ⓑ _____

    _____

3. **What place in the Americas or Antarctica do you want to visit?**
    (Your Supporting Idea 3)

    _____

    What would you see and do there? (Details)

    Ⓐ _____

    _____

    Ⓑ _____

    _____

4. **What are your feelings about the places you want to visit?**
    (Your Concluding Sentence)

    _____

    _____

    _____

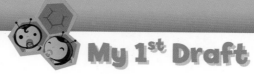

My 1st Draft

Rewrite your ideas from the previous pages in complete sentences.

Title

Places I Want to Visit

Topic Sentence

There are many _____ places in the world that I want to see, and someday _____.

Body

_____

_____

_____

_____

_____

_____

_____

_____

_____

_____

Concluding Sentence

_____

_____

✔**Peer Proofreading Checklist:**

☐ **Punctuation** ✔capitalization ✔commas(,) ✔periods(.) ✔question marks(?)

☐ **Correct spelling**

☐ **Complete sentences** S + V + end of sentence

Switch books with your partner and proofread your partner's writing.

↳ After proofreading your 1st draft, rewrite it on your final draft.

Fun Quiz

Q: At the top of page 52, what is the boy carrying around his neck?

A: It _____. <Answer Key p. 80>

A Strange/Funny Happening

Writing Prompt

A. Read the writing prompt carefully. Then circle the important words.

> Do you know someone who had something very strange or funny happen to him or her? Who was the person? When and where did it happen? What was the incident? Why or how did it happen?

Topic Sentence

B. Think of a strange or funny story that happened to someone and write your answers.

Q: What is the strangest or funniest story you have ever heard? Who did the incident happen to?

The strangest/funniest story I have ever heard  happened to _____

when _____.

- a friend, a boy/girl I know, my brother/sister, a boy/girl in my school, a boy/girl in my neighborhood, (name/names of the person/people)
- he/she fell down on the wet floor in the bathroom
- he/she fell and bumped his/her head
- he/she had an accident in the bathroom
- he/she was walking home late one night
- he/she said he/she saw a ghost

C. Ask and answer the following questions with your partner. Then add one more idea in each of the boxes. **‹ Supporting Ideas**

Q: When and where did it happen?

It **happened** to him/her **yesterday at school.**

When

- yesterday
- a week ago
- a month ago
- a year ago
-

- two days ago
- three weeks ago
- six months ago
- two years ago

Where

- at school
- at home
- at a park
- on the street
- in a cemetery
-

- in the classroom
- at a restaurant
- at the playground
- at a shopping mall

Q: How did the incident begin?

He/She **was** **late and in a hurry** to get to (the place: _____).

- was late for class, so he/she was running down the hall as fast as he/she could
- likes to read books all the time and doesn't know what is happening around him/her
- raised his/her hand and asked the teacher if he/she could go to the bathroom
- went to his/her friend's house to play computer games
-

A. Talk about the pictures. Then read the story.

A Funny Happening: The Sleepwalker

A very embarrassing thing happened to Jimmy Jones, a fourth-grader at Oak Tree Elementary School, when he woke up one night in a strange place. The incident happened to him three days ago in his neighborhood on Elm Street. Jimmy played soccer that day and was so exhausted that he went to bed right after dinner. At around midnight, Jimmy got up, went down the stairs, and walked out the front door. He then walked next door to the home of the Smith family and knocked really loudly on the front door. Mrs. Smith, who was watching TV at the time, was frightened by the loud noise. She thought it was a burglar. But when she went to the front door and looked through the peephole on the door, she realized it was Jimmy from next door. He was sleepwalking. When Mrs. Smith opened the door, Jimmy woke up. He was really confused because he had no idea why he was at his neighbor's house. Jimmy was really embarrassed and just wanted to disappear somewhere.

B. Discuss the questions about the story.

- What happened to Jimmy Jones one night?
- When and where did it happen?
- What happened first?
- What happened next?
- What happened last?

Topic Sentence

a very embarrassing thing happened to Jimmy Jones, woke up in a strange place

When	Why/How		
	First	**Next**	**Last**
three days ago	was exhausted → played soccer, went to bed right after dinner → got up at midnight	went to his neighbor's house → knocked loudly on the door, frightened Mrs. Smith → Mrs. Smith thought it was a burglar	scared Mrs. Smith → realized it was Jimmy sleepwalking → opened the door, Jimmy woke up confused

Where

in his neighborhood

Concluding Sentence

Jimmy was embarrassed and just wanted to disappear somewhere.

Key Vocabulary & Expressions

- fourth-grader(s), incident(s), neighborhood(s), midnight, stair(s), burglar(s), peephole(s), neighbor(s)
- knock/knocked, realize/realized, sleepwalk/sleepwalked, disappear/disappeared
- embarrassing, embarrassed, exhausted, frightened, confused

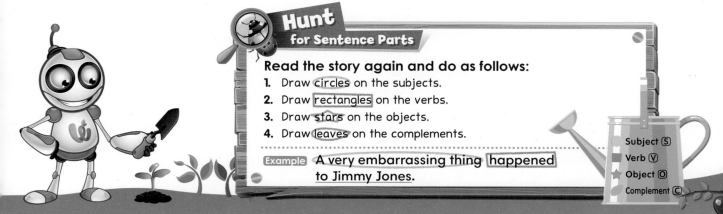

Hunt for Sentence Parts

Read the story again and do as follows:
1. Draw circles on the subjects.
2. Draw rectangles on the verbs.
3. Draw stars on the objects.
4. Draw leaves on the complements.

Example   A very embarrassing thing happened to Jimmy Jones.

Subject Ⓢ
Verb Ⓥ
Object Ⓞ
Complement Ⓒ

61

Writing Process

 **Planning**

Brainstorm and write your ideas. Any idea is all right.

_____

_____

_____

_____

Topic
A Strange/
Funny Happening

_____

_____

_____

 Gathering & Organizing

Gather and organize your ideas in the correct spaces. For your topic sentence and supporting ideas, you can use the phrases on *Writing Prompt* (pp. 58–59).

Topic: A Strange/Funny Happening

Topic Sentence
A very strange/funny thing happened to _____ when _____.

When	Why/How		
	First	**Next**	**Last**
_____ _____	_____ _____ _____ _____ _____	_____ _____ _____ _____ _____	_____ _____ _____ _____ _____
Where			
_____ _____			

Concluding Sentence
He/She felt really _____ and wanted to _____.

Adding Details

Here are some example details for your supporting ideas. ‹ Details

First

- My friend was late for class, so she was running down the hall as fast as she could. Also, she was carrying a heavy book bag. She heard the bell ring, so she tried to run even faster.
- My sister likes to read books all the time and doesn't know what is happening around her. Sometimes she reads them while she's walking. One day, she was reading a book on her way to school.
- He/She raised his/her hand and asked the teacher if he/she could go to the bathroom. The teacher gave him/her a permission slip and excused him/her from the class. He/She walked out the door of the classroom as the other students watched him/her.
- It was the first day of summer vacation, so he/she went to his/her friend's house to play computer games. They played computer games all day long, and they finally stopped at dinnertime. His/Her friend's mother invited him/her to have dinner with them, and he/she did.

Next

- In front of her was another student who was also late for class. He was running, too. Then he stopped suddenly to tie his shoelace.
- That morning, workers made a new sidewalk with fresh concrete. They were still working on the sidewalk when my sister came along. She was not watching where she was going and happened to step into the wet concrete.
- He/She was in the bathroom for a long time. Finally, he/she was finished and he/she washed his/her hands and came out. Then he/she went back down the hall to his/her classroom, opened the door, and went in as quietly as he/she could.
- After dinner, he/she said good night and started walking home. It was six blocks to his/her house, and he/she had to pass the cemetery. He/She was a little scared because he/she believed in ghosts and thought there might be a ghost in the cemetery.

Last

- But my friend couldn't stop, so she fell on top of the boy, and they both were lying on the floor. The other students were very surprised by the big noise. Then they all started to laugh at my friend and the boy.
- My sister was really enjoying the book, and she didn't know she was walking in wet concrete. The workers yelled at her, and she stopped reading. Then she looked down and saw the wet concrete around her ankles.
- As soon as he/she walked into the classroom, everyone started laughing. He/She had no idea what they were laughing at. When he/she turned around to look behind him/her, he/she saw that a piece of toilet paper was stuck to the back of his/her pants/skirt/dress.
- Just as he/she was passing the cemetery, he/she saw a green light rising from a grave. The hair on his/her neck stood up and he/she was terrified. He/She started to run as fast as he/she could and ran all the way home without stopping.

Feelings — Your Concluding Sentence

- He/She was so ashamed of what he/she had done and felt terrible about it.
- His/Her face turned red, and he/she felt so embarrassed because of what he/she did.
- He/She was so embarrassed that he/she wanted to run away and hide.
- He/She just stood there and couldn't believe his/her eyes.
- He/She said it was the most embarrassing thing that ever happened to him/her, but now he/she laughs about it.
- Nobody can say for sure what he/she saw that night, but it is something he/she will never forget.

Answer the questions below. You can write your own answers or choose from the examples on the previous page.

1. **What happened first?** (Details)

   (A) _____

   _____

   (B) _____

   _____

   (C) _____

   _____

2. **What happened next?** (Details)

   (A) _____

   _____

   (B) _____

   _____

   (C) _____

   _____

3. **What happened last?** (Details)

   (A) _____

   _____

   (B) _____

   _____

   (C) _____

   _____

4. **What were his/her feelings about the strange/funny happening?**
   (Your Concluding Sentence)

   _____

   _____

   _____

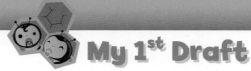 **My 1ˢᵗ Draft**

Rewrite your ideas from the previous pages in complete sentences.

Title

A Strange/Funny Happening

Topic Sentence

A very strange/funny thing happened to _____

when _____ .

Body

_____

_____

_____

_____

_____

_____

_____

_____

_____

Concluding Sentence

_____

_____

✔ **Peer Proofreading Checklist:**

☐ **Punctuation** ✔capitalization ✔commas(,) ✔periods(.) ✔question marks(?)

☐ **Correct spelling**

☐ **Complete sentences** S + V + end of sentence

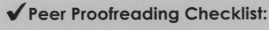 Switch books with your partner and proofread your partner's writing.

➤ After proofreading your 1ˢᵗ draft, rewrite it on your final draft.

Fun Quiz

Q: In the picture on the bottom of page 60, what is in the woman's left hand?

A: It _____ . <Answer Key p. 80>

The Best Job in the World

Writing Prompt

A. Read the writing prompt carefully. Then circle the important words.

What do you want to be when you grow up?
What do you think is the best job in the world?
Why do you feel that way? Write about
your favorite job and give reasons for
your opinion.

Topic Sentence

B. Think of your own best job in the world and write your answer.

Q: What do you want to be when you grow up?

When I grow up, I want to be _____

because I think it is the best job in the world.

• an artist	• an inventor	• a scientist	• a doctor
• a fashion designer	• a chef	• a musician	• a lawyer
• a teacher	• a vet	• a police officer	• a firefighter
• an astronaut	• a pilot		

C. Ask and answer the following questions with your partner. Then add one more idea in each of the boxes. **Supporting Ideas**

Q: Why do you think it is the best job in the world?

It ___ is ___ because **the job looks like a lot of fun**.

Enjoyable

- the job looks like a lot of fun
- the job would be very fun and exciting
- this is a very exciting and adventurous job
- I enjoy creative work
- I like helping people
- I enjoy using my imagination
- I love entertaining people
- _____

Respectable

- everyone thinks this job is cool
- this is a very respectable job
- people would always look up to me
- everybody thinks this is a very important job
- most people think this job is admirable
- _____

Profitable

- I would make a lot of money
- I could become rich and famous
- the job pays well
- I would earn a good salary
- the pay is fantastic
- I can make a pretty good salary
- _____

A. Talk about the pictures. Then read the story.

The Best Job in the World

When I grow up, I want to be a pilot because I think it is the best job in the world. First of all, it would be very fun and exciting to become a pilot. Pilots control a huge and heavy airplane from a cockpit, and they make it go up high into the air. Also, they can fly their airplanes and travel to many faraway and wonderful places around the world. The second thing is that many people think pilots are so cool. Pilots wear a uniform and a hat, which make them look very nice and sharp. Moreover, pilots get to fly an airplane high above the clouds, and not everyone has the chance to experience something like that. Last of all, many pilots make a lot of money. Pilots are well paid because they receive special training for a long time. Pilots can have a very comfortable life with a good salary. I know that becoming a pilot is not very easy, but I will study hard and do my best to achieve my goal someday.

B. Discuss the questions about the story.

- What does the girl want to be when she grows up?
- What is the girl's first reason?
- What is the girl's second reason?
- What is the girl's third reason?

Topic Sentence

when I grow up, want to be a pilot

Enjoyable

fun and exciting
→ control a huge and heavy airplane from a cockpit
→ can fly their airplanes and travel to faraway and wonderful places

Respectable

people think pilots are so cool
→ wear a uniform and a hat
→ get to fly an airplane high above the clouds

Profitable

pilots make a lot of money
→ well paid because they receive special training for a long time
→ can have a comfortable life with a good salary

Concluding Sentence

will study hard and do my best to achieve my goal

Key Vocabulary & Expressions

- pilot(s), cockpit(s), uniform(s), cloud(s), training, salary (salaries), goal(s)
- control/controlled, pay/paid, receive/received, achieve/achieved
- sharp, comfortable   • faraway

Hunt for Sentence Parts

Read the story again and do as follows:
1. Draw circles on the subjects.
2. Draw rectangles on the verbs.
3. Draw stars on the objects.
4. Draw leaves on the complements.

Example When I grow up, I want to be a pilot.

Subject S
Verb V
Object O
Complement C

69

Planning

Brainstorm and write your ideas. Any idea is all right.

Topic
The Best Job
in the World

Gathering & Organizing

Gather and organize your ideas in the correct spaces. For your topic sentence and supporting ideas, you can use the phrases on *Writing Prompt* (pp. 66–67).

Topic: The Best Job in the World

Topic Sentence
When I grow up, I want to be _____ because I think it is the best job in the world.

Enjoyable	Respectable	Profitable
It is because _____	It is because _____	It is because _____

Concluding Sentence
_____ to achieve my goal someday.

Adding Details

Here are some example details for your supporting ideas. ‹ **Details**

Enjoyable

- Artists create works of art that make them very proud.
- Inventors enjoy making things that improve our lives.
- Scientists experience great satisfaction from finding new and important things in their research.
- Doctors have great satisfaction from making people well.
- Chefs are happy when people enjoy their food.
- Musicians love it when people appreciate their music.
- Lawyers feel good about helping people with their problems.
- Teachers feel very important when students learn new things.
- Vets feel a great sense of love and compassion towards the animals they treat.
- Police officers feel very good about helping keep people safe.
- Firefighters are very happy when they put out a fire or rescue people from burning buildings.
- Astronauts are thrilled to be able to go into space in a spacecraft.

Respectable

- They create art/music that is a very important part of our culture.
- They are respected by everyone for the work they do in making the world a better place.
- They are recognized for their genius and for making our world a better place to live.
- People appreciate all that they do in performing a dangerous and difficult service to society.
- People really appreciate the things they do for everyone.
- They do very important work and look really nice in their uniforms.
- People feel very proud when they see them in uniform.
- They have the deep respect of their students for the things they teach them.
- Their ability to create new and useful things is admired by everyone.
- They are some of the most respected public servants.
- People often praise them for the public service they perform.

Profitable

- They work very hard and are paid well for their efforts.
- They earn a lot of money because the job is difficult and dangerous.
- They are paid very well because few people can do this type of work.
- They make a lot of money because they have to study for years to learn their skills.
- They make enough money to live a comfortable life.
- They make so much money they have trouble spending it.
- They are paid a huge bonus at the end of each year.
- They make more in one month than some people make in one year.

Feelings — Your Concluding Sentence

- I will do my very best to achieve my goal someday.
- I will study hard and try my best to achieve my goal someday.
- I will work as hard as I can to reach my goal someday.

Answer the questions below. You can write your own answers or choose from the examples on the previous page.

1. **What would you enjoy about this job?** (Your Supporting Idea 1)

    _____

    Write two more sentences about why you would enjoy the job. (Details)

    Ⓐ _____

    _____

    Ⓑ _____

    _____

2. **How respectable is this job?** (Your Supporting Idea 2)

    _____

    Write two more sentences about the job's respectability. (Details)

    Ⓐ _____

    _____

    Ⓑ _____

    _____

3. **How well does this job pay?** (Your Supporting Idea 3)

    _____

    Write two more sentences about the pay. (Details)

    Ⓐ _____

    _____

    Ⓑ _____

    _____

4. **What are your feelings about achieving your goal?**
    (Your Concluding Sentence)

    _____

    _____

    _____

 **My 1ˢᵗ Draft**

Rewrite your ideas from the previous pages in complete sentences.

Title

The Best Job in the World

Topic Sentence

When I grow up, I want to be _____ because
I think it is the best job in the world.

Body

_____

_____

_____

_____

_____

_____

_____

_____

_____

Concluding Sentence

_____

_____

✔ **Peer Proofreading Checklist:**

☐ **Punctuation** ✔capitalization ✔commas(,) ✔periods(.) ✔question marks(?)

☐ **Correct spelling**

☐ **Complete sentences** S + V + end of sentence

Switch books with your partner and proofread your partner's writing.

↳ After proofreading your 1ˢᵗ draft, rewrite it on your final draft.

Fun Quiz

Q: How many airplanes do you see on page 68?

A: There _____ . <Answer Key p. 80>

73

Review Units 5 & 6

A. Write the past tense.

1. earn _____

2. grow _____

3. recognize _____

4. win _____

5. have/has _____

6. travel _____

7. hope _____

8. lean _____

9. measure _____

10. experience _____

B. Complete the topic and concluding sentences using the phrases from the box below.

1. It would be wonderful if I grew up _____

_____.

2. I can't wait to visit these places _____

_____.

3. There are many famous places in the world that I want _____

_____.

4. Figure skating is my favorite sport, and I want to be like Kim Yuna, _____

_____.

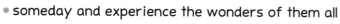

- someday and experience the wonders of them all
- who is a South Korean figure skater
- to be like Kim Yuna, who is almost perfect in every way
- to see, and someday I hope to visit a few of them

C. Write the proper supporting ideas from the box below.

1. _____

The Tower of Pisa there is famous because it is leaning to one side at an angle of about four degrees. I want to go to the Tower of Pisa and actually measure it for myself.

2. _____

She earns a lot of money from competitions and advertising. Moreover, she is so famous that fans follow her everywhere.

3. _____

I am fascinated by the Great Sphinx of Giza, which is a large stone lion with a man's head. Seeing the Great Sphinx of Giza in Egypt would be a dream come true.

4. _____

Her skating is so beautiful, graceful, and powerful. Also, she has won many medals, including a gold medal at the 2010 Winter Olympic Games.

5. _____

She donates a lot of money to charity. In addition, she is a UNICEF Goodwill Ambassador and helps people in need around the world.

6. _____

The Great Wall of China is more than 2,300 years old, and it is the longest man-made structure in the world. It would be very exciting to walk along the top of the Great Wall of China.

- The last place I want to travel to is Italy.
- Another place I want to go to is China.
- One place that I want to visit is Egypt.
- The second reason that I want to be like Kim Yuna is because she is very rich and famous.
- The first reason that I want to be like Kim Yuna is because she is one of the greatest female figure skaters in the world.
- The last reason that I want to be like Kim Yuna is because she has a warm and generous heart.

sticker

 Activity cards are available at the back of the book.

Review Units 7 & 8

A. Write the past tense.

1. think _____
2. sleepwalk _____
3. happen _____
4. wake _____
5. disappear _____

6. control _____
7. fly _____
8. pay _____
9. receive _____
10. achieve _____

B. Complete the topic and concluding sentences using the phrases from the box below.

1. A very embarrassing thing happened to Jimmy Jones, a fourth-grader at Oak

   Tree _____.

2. When I grow up, I want to be a pilot because I _____

   _____.

3. I know that becoming a pilot is not very easy, but _____

   _____.

4. Jimmy was really _____

   _____.

- Elementary School, when he woke up one night in a strange place
- I will study hard and do my best to achieve my goal someday
- embarrassed and just wanted to disappear somewhere
- think it is the best job in the world

C. Write the proper supporting ideas from the box below.

1. _____

   She thought it was a burglar. But when she went to the front door and looked through the peephole on the door, she realized it was Jimmy from next door.

2. _____

   Pilots wear a uniform and a hat, which make them look very nice and sharp. Moreover, pilots get to fly an airplane high above the clouds, and not everyone has the chance to experience something like that.

3. _____

   When Mrs. Smith opened the door, Jimmy woke up. He was really confused because he had no idea why he was at his neighbor's house.

4. _____

   Pilots are well paid because they receive special training for a long time. Pilots can have a very comfortable life with a good salary.

5. _____

   Jimmy played soccer that day and was so exhausted that he went to bed right after dinner. At around midnight, Jimmy got up, went down the stairs, and walked out the front door.

6. _____

   Pilots control a huge and heavy airplane from a cockpit, and they make it go up high into the air. Also, they can fly their airplanes and travel to many faraway and wonderful places around the world.

- First of all, it would be very fun and exciting to become a pilot.
- Last of all, many pilots make a lot of money.
- Mrs. Smith, who was watching TV at the time, was frightened by the loud noise.
- The incident happened to him three days ago in his neighborhood on Elm Street.
- The second thing is that many people think pilots are so cool.
- He was sleepwalking.

 Activity cards are available at the back of the book.

Writing Help

Conjunctions for Connecting Sentences

Conjunctions	Examples
because (reason)	Because we were having so much fun, time went by really quickly. Time went by really quickly because we were having so much fun.
if (condition)	If I could visit Europe, it would be the best experience ever. It would be the best experience ever if I could visit Europe.
when (time)	When I grow up, I want to be a pilot. I want to be a pilot when I grow up.
so that (purpose)	The robot would teach me many things so that I would become a genius.
so...that (result)	I got so excited that I fell in the water.
that (noun clause)	I hope that we can do it again someday. (used as an object)

Adjectives for Quantity and Amount

Meaning	With countable nouns	With uncountable nouns
a lot of, lots of	many There were so many fun rides.	much She gets so much money from advertising.
a small number or amount of	a few I hope to visit a few famous places.	a little We only had a little money to spend for our vacation.
almost nothing	few Few people can do it.	little The charity has little money left, so they need help.

* *A lot of* and *lots of* are used with both countable and uncountable nouns.
   There were a lot of (lots of) <u>activities</u> we could enjoy. (with a countable noun)
   I could save a lot of (lots of) <u>time</u>. (with an uncountable noun)

Confusing Adjectives: verb + -ing vs. verb + -ed

A verb + -ing (present participle) describes the people or things that cause the feelings.	A verb + -ed (past participle) tells how people feel.
We saw amazing old buildings.	We were amazed by the old buildings.
The movie was boring.	I was bored during the last class.
It was an embarrassing moment.	He was embarrassed that night.
The pyramids were fascinating.	I was fascinated by the pyramids.
The noise was so frightening.	She was frightened by the noise.
Natural history is interesting.	I am interested in natural history.
The news was very surprising.	We were surprised at the news.

 ## Options for Overused Words

good		nice		bad	
amazing	awesome	enjoyable	lovely	awful	poor
excellent	super	helpful	friendly	naughty	terrible
fantastic	wonderful	kind	admirable	horrible	mean

sad		happy		scared	
depressed	unhappy	pleased	glad	afraid	frightened
sorrowful	upset	cheerful	excited	fearful	shaken
miserable	tearful	thrilled	delighted	startled	terrified

big		little		pretty	
gigantic	huge	small	tiny	beautiful	cute
enormous	large	petite	miniature	attractive	lovely

said		ran		like	
replied	shouted	hurried	dashed	enjoy	appreciate
whispered	responded	rushed	raced	admire	respect
explained	exclaimed	skipped	jogged	treasure	fancy

Answer Key

Unit 1 A Day with Dad/Mom ▶p.13

Fun Quiz: How many fish did the boy on page 8 catch?
A: He caught (only) one fish.

Unit 2 The Money Tree ▶p.21

Fun Quiz: In the picture at the top of page 16, what is the girl under the tree doing?
A: She is picking the paper money.

Unit 3 The Best Vacation Ever ▶p.29

Fun Quiz: On page 24, how many people are paddling the raft?
A: There are six. (The person in the white helmet is guiding, not paddling.)

Unit 4 Three Wishes ▶p.37

Fun Quiz: In the picture on page 32, how many legs does the cleaning robot have?
A: It has six legs.

Unit 5 A Sports Star I Want to Be Like ▶p.49

Fun Quiz: On page 44, what does the girl in the blue shirt have around her neck?
A: It is a necklace.

Unit 6 Places I Want to Visit ▶p.57

Fun Quiz: At the top of page 52, what is the boy carrying around his neck?
A: It is a camera.

Unit 7 A Strange/Funny Happening ▶p.65

Fun Quiz: In the picture on the bottom of page 60, what is in the woman's left hand?
A: It is a doorknob.

Unit 8 The Best Job in The World ▶p.73

Fun Quiz: How many airplanes do you see on page 68?
A: There are three. (There is one more airplane on the magazine.)

S	V		
I	spent	an unforgettable day	with my mom, who is the most caring person I know.
My best friend and I	spent	an unforgettable day	with my dad, who is the greatest person in the world.
Leona and Sunny	want	to spend the day doing something exciting	during their vacation.
Betty	was able to spend	a memorable day	with her mom, who is the most important person in her life.
Sue	would like to spend	a whole day	with just her dad, who is the greatest person in the world.
Betty and Sue	would like to see	a rainbow	high in the sky.
Most of my Malaysian friends	will see	snow-covered mountains	for the first time.
Jena and May	saw	beautiful eagles flying	high above the lake.
Jessie	wanted	to see the fantastic views of the rocky canyon walls	during the daytime.

Writing Garden Book 3

Writing Garden Book 3

Writing Garden Book 3

Writing Garden Book 3

Writing Garden Book 3

Writing Garden Book 3

Writing Garden Book 3

Writing Garden Book 3

Writing Garden Book 3

Writing Garden Book 3

Writing Garden Book 3

Writing Garden Book 3

Writing Garden Book 3

Writing Garden Book 3

Writing Garden Book 3

Writing Garden Book 3

Writing Garden Book 3

Writing Garden Book 3

Writing Garden Book 3

Writing Garden Book 3

Writing Garden Book 3

Writing Garden Book 3

Writing Garden Book 3

Writing Garden Book 3

Writing Garden Book 3

Caroline and Sarah	would like to build	a campfire	by the tent at night.
Reina and Elina	built	hospitals	for people who have no money.
Stacy and Irene	will build	social centers	for elderly people.
Dana and Hanna	would like to use	the money	to help abandoned or abused animals.
Jennifer and Kate	would like to donate	most of the money	to help poor people.
Juliet and Alex	wanted	to donate lots of money	to children in need.
Erica and Gladys	donated	money	to help people who are elderly and lonely.
Jason and Bella	will donate	their money	to help people who don't have homes.
Justin and Amanda	are going to donate	a lot of money	to build schools for poor children.

Writing Garden Book 3

Writing Garden Book 3

Writing Garden Book 3

Writing Garden Book 3

Writing Garden Book 3

Writing Garden Book 3

Writing Garden Book 3

Writing Garden Book 3

Writing Garden Book 3

Writing Garden Book 3

Writing Garden Book 3

Writing Garden Book 3

Writing Garden Book 3

Writing Garden Book 3

Writing Garden Book 3

Writing Garden Book 3

Writing Garden Book 3

Writing Garden Book 3

Writing Garden Book 3

Writing Garden Book 3

Writing Garden Book 3

Writing Garden Book 3

Writing Garden Book 3

Writing Garden Book 3

Writing Garden Book 3

Writing Garden Book 3

Writing Garden Book 3

Writing Garden Book 3

Writing Garden Book 3

Writing Garden Book 3

Writing Garden Book 3

Writing Garden Book 3

Writing Garden Book 3

Writing Garden Book 3

Writing Garden Book 3

Writing Garden Book 3

S	V	O	
John and Sue	can have	many more wonderful family vacations like that	in the future.
Jasmine and Jessica	had	a great time	together enjoying the wonders of nature.
Betty	had	such a great time	that the vacation was over before she knew it.
June and Billy	would like to take	many trips	all over the world.
Lauren and Jin	wanted	to take a special trip	to get to know each other.
Jessie and May	can have	a very comfortable life	with a good salary.
Susan and Vicky	can't wait	to visit these places of wonder and beauty	someday.
Joy	would like to visit	Europe	someday.
My plan	is	to visit all of these famous places	within the next five years.

Writing Garden Book 3

Writing Garden Book 3

Writing Garden Book 3

Writing Garden Book 3

Writing Garden Book 3

Writing Garden Book 3

Writing Garden Book 3

Writing Garden Book 3

Writing Garden Book 3

Writing Garden Book 3

Writing Garden Book 3

Writing Garden Book 3

Writing Garden Book 3

Writing Garden Book 3

Writing Garden Book 3

Writing Garden Book 3

Writing Garden Book 3

Writing Garden Book 3

Writing Garden Book 3

Writing Garden Book 3

Writing Garden Book 3

Writing Garden Book 3

Writing Garden Book 3

Writing Garden Book 3

Writing Garden Book 3

Writing Garden Book 3

Writing Garden Book 3

Subject	Verb	Object	Phrase
Gina and Heather	want	to visit Egypt	to see the Great Sphinx of Giza.
Lia and Anna	would like to visit	China	to see the Great Wall of China.
Ashley and Gen	visited	Italy	to see the Tower of Pisa.
Tony and Paul	will visit	the United States	to see the Statue of Liberty.
Nicky and Julie	make	a lot of money	because they have skills that required many years of study.
Lucy and Judith	will make	enough money	to live a comfortable life.
David and Stella	made	so much money	that they can live happily for a lifetime.
Jason and Kate	want	to make more money	than other people.
Monica and Noah	would like to make	lots of money	so they can become rich and famous.

Writing Garden Book 3

Writing Garden Book 3

Writing Garden Book 3

Writing Garden Book 3

Writing Garden Book 3

Writing Garden Book 3

Writing Garden Book 3

Writing Garden Book 3

Writing Garden Book 3

Writing Garden Book 3

Writing Garden Book 3

Writing Garden Book 3

Writing Garden Book 3

Writing Garden Book 3

Writing Garden Book 3

Writing Garden Book 3

Writing Garden Book 3

Writing Garden Book 3

Writing Garden Book 3

Writing Garden Book 3

Writing Garden Book 3

Writing Garden Book 3

Writing Garden Book 3

Writing Garden Book 3

Writing Garden Book 3

Writing Garden Book 3

Writing Garden Book 3

Writing Garden Book 3

Writing Garden Book 3

Writing Garden Book 3

Writing Garden Book 3

Writing Garden Book 3

Writing Garden Book 3

Writing Garden Book 3

Writing Garden Book 3

Writing Garden Book 3

Writing Garden Book 3

Writing Garden Book 3

Writing Garden Book 3

Writing Garden Book 3

Review Stickers

▶ page 39

▶ page 41

▶ page 75

▶ page 77

Writing Garden

Workbook 3

J. Randolph Lewis

Lucy Han

Helen Kim

Paragraph Writing

What are drones, and what can they
do like flying robots.

Writing Garden 3
Written by J. Randolph Lewis, Lucy Han, Helen Kim

Publisher: Anna Park

Project Director: Lucy Han

Content Editor: Kelli Ripatti, Sherry Lee

Designer: Eun Jee Kang

Illustrators: Beehive Illustration (Beatrice Bencivenni, John Lund, Philip Hailstone)

Cover Design: Hongdangmoo

Printer: Kyujang TPC

ISBN: 979-11-87999-01-0
Photo Credits:
Photos and images © Shutterstock, Inc.

www.runningturtle.co.kr
1203, 36, Hwangsaeul-ro 200beon-gil, Bundang-gu, Seongnam-si, Gyeonggi-do, KOREA 13595
TEL: +82-2-3452-7979 FAX: +82-31-718-3452

KC This book has been printed with non-toxic materials.

Writing Garden

Workbook 3

Language **Sprouts**

🌱 Sentence Practice

Combine the sentences using the conjunction *that*.

The conjuction *that* connects sentences.

I got <u>very excited</u>. <u>As a result</u>, I fell in the water.

= I got **so excited** that I fell in the water.

so + Adjective/Adverb   Conjunction   (*that*-clause shows the result)

We can do it again someday. <u>I hope</u> we will.

= I hope **that** we can do it again someday.

          Conjunction   (*that*-clause is like a noun)

---

1. We were <u>very full</u>. <u>As a result</u>, we couldn't eat another bite.

    <u>We were so full that we couldn't eat another bite</u>   .

2. It was <u>so much fun</u>. <u>As a result</u>, I want to do it again.

    _____ .

3. The fish I caught was <u>very big</u>. <u>As a result</u>, I could not get it into the boat.

    _____

    _____ .

4. We ate <u>so much</u>. <u>As a result</u>, we thought our stomachs were going to pop.

    _____ .

5. My mom is the most wonderful person in the world. That is what <u>I think</u>.

    I _____ .

6. Going camping could be so much fun. That is what <u>my mom thinks</u>.

My mom _____.

7. My dad is a good cook. <u>I found</u> that <u>out</u>.

I _____.

8. We roasted marshmallows on the fire. <u>I remember</u> that.

I _____.

9. We learned a lot from each other. <u>I think</u> so.

I _____.

10. There were many fascinating exhibitions in the museum. <u>My mom said</u> so.

My _____

_____.

🌱 Revising Practice

Correct the underlined words. Rewrite the sentences.

1. I spent the whole day with my mom, who <u>are</u> the greatest person I know.
(Subject-Verb Agreement)

_____.

2. My dad jumped in the lake and <u>save</u> me like a superhero. (Tense)

_____.

3. I spent <u>a</u> unforgettable day with my parents. (Word Form)

_____.

4. We had so much <u>funny</u> that we laughed so hard. (Word Form)

_____.

Expanding Sentences

Expand the sentences below by answering the questions using the given words.

> **Example:** We went fishing.
>
> ● **Who?**   My dad and I went fishing.
> ● **What?**   My dad and I went catfish fishing.
> ● **Where?** My dad and I went fishing at a lake.
> ● **When?**   My dad and I went fishing at a lake in the afternoon.
> ● **Why?**   My dad and I went fishing at a lake to catch some fish for dinner.

The boy spent a day with his dad.

1. Who? (My best friend)

   _____

2. What? (spent an unforgettable day)

   _____

3. Where? (in the mountains)

   _____

4. When? (last Saturday)

   _____

   _____

5. Why? (to try to have a closer relationship with his dad)

   _____

   _____

   _____

Title: A Day with Dad/Mom

_____ , I spent a special day

with my dad/mom, who is _____ .

_____

_____

_____

_____

_____

_____

_____

_____

_____

_____

_____

_____

_____

_____

_____

_____

<More Than 170 Words>

| My Comment | ☐ Good | |
| | ☐ Excellent | |

| Parent's Comment | ☐ Good | ☐ Excellent |
| Teacher's Comment | ☐ Good | ☐ Excellent |

🌱 Sentence Practice

Make conditional sentences using *If...would* + verb.

Conditionals for unreal situations: *if* + past tense...*would* + verb

If you found a money tree, what would you do?
If I found a money tree, I **would buy** a big house.
If Past Tense   *would* + Verb

= I **would buy** a big house **if** I **found** a money tree.
(It is impossible to find a money tree, though.)

1. I become rich. I donate money to children in need.

   If I became rich, I would donate money to children in need   .

2. I become very rich. I build schools for poor children.

   If _____.

3. We go to France. We visit the Eiffel Tower.

   If _____.

4. I find a money tree. I use the money for myself.

   If _____.

5. I donate money to a charity. They use the money to build schools for children.

   If _____

   _____.

6. I build a house. It has a big swimming pool.

_____

_____.

7. I spend money from a money tree on charity. It is rewarding.

_____

_____.

8. I buy an airplane with that money. My family travels around the world.

_____

_____.

🌱 Revising Practice

Correct the underlined words. Rewrite the sentences.

1. There <u>is</u> so many hungry children in the world. (Subject-Verb Agreement)

_____.

2. If I found a money tree, I <u>will</u> use the money for myself. (Tense)

_____.

3. I would go on a trip to many foreign <u>country</u>. (Word Form)

_____.

4. <u>Finally</u> I would get a nice car for my parents. (Punctuation)

_____.

Expanding Sentences

Expand the sentences below by answering the questions using the given words.

Example: The girl found a money tree.

- **Who?** My best friend, Sue, found a money tree.
- **What?** My best friend, Sue, found a money tree covered in 100-dollar bills.
- **Where?** My best friend, Sue, found a money tree covered in 100-dollar bills in her backyard.
- **When?** My best friend, Sue, found a money tree covered in 100-dollar bills in her backyard last night.
- **How?** My best friend, Sue, found a money tree covered in 100-dollar bills in her backyard last night when it magically appeared in front of her.

The girl donated money to charity.

1. Who? (The warm-hearted girl)

_____

2. What? (donated a lot of money)

_____

3. Where? (in Africa)

_____

4. When? (as soon as she gathered a large basketful of money from the money tree in her backyard)

_____

_____

5. Why? (so poor children could get a good education and have a better future)

_____

_____

_____

My Final Draft

Title: The Money Tree

If I found a money tree, I would use the money for

<More Than 170 Words>

My Comment ☐ Good ☐ Excellent

Parent's Comment ☐ Good ☐ Excellent
Teacher's Comment ☐ Good ☐ Excellent

🌱 Sentence Practice

Combine the sentences using the conjunction *and* or *but*.

The conjuctions *and* and *but* connect sentences.

I spent three days with my family in the Grand Canyon. Spending three days with my family in the Grand Canyon was the best vacation I've ever had.

= I spent three days with my family in the Grand Canyon, **and** it was the best vacation I've ever had.

The experience was physically exhausting. I think it made me a better person.

= The experience was physically exhausting, **but** I think it made me a better person.

1. My family hiked down a steep trail. My family went to the bottom of the canyon. (and)

    My family hiked down a steep trail, and we went to the bottom of the
    canyon   .

2. My family enjoyed swimming in the ocean. My sister made many sandcastles on the beach. (and)

    _____

    _____ .

3. We didn't say a word during the hike because we were exhausted. We were really touched by the power and the beauty of nature. (but)

    _____

    _____ .

4. We talked a lot during the trip. We laughed a lot during the trip. (and)

    _____

    _____ .

5. The mountains and the trees were amazing. The blue ocean with the shiny beach was more amazing. (but)

_____

_____.

6. We rode a raft. We paddled down the Colorado River. (and)

_____

_____.

7. I thought that spending time with friends was more exciting. I realized that spending time with my family was the most exciting. (but)

_____

_____.

8. I enjoyed hiking to the top of the mountain. I was more excited about rafting down the river. (but)

_____

_____.

🌱 Revising Practice

Correct the underlined words. Rewrite the sentences.

1. There <u>was</u> so many great activities we could enjoy in the Grand Canyon.
(Subject-Verb Agreement)

_____.

2. My family hiked down a steep trail and <u>go</u> to the bottom of the canyon. (Tense)

_____.

3. We even watched a <u>beauty</u> sunset in the evening. (Word Form)

_____.

4. I hope we can have <u>much</u> more wonderful family vacations like that. (Word Form)

_____.

 **Expanding Sentences**

Expand the sentences below by answering the questions using the given words.

Example: The boy spent three days with his family.

- **Who?** The fourth-grade boy spent three days with his family.
- **What?** The fourth-grade boy spent three exciting days on vacation with his family.
- **Where?** The fourth-grade boy spent three exciting days on vacation with his family in the Grand Canyon.
- **When?** The fourth-grade boy spent three exciting days on vacation with his family in the Grand Canyon last summer.
- **Why?** The fourth-grade boy spent three exciting days on vacation with his family in the Grand Canyon last summer so they could enjoy nature together.

We hiked down a trail.

1. Who? (My best friend and I)

   _____

2. What? (hiked down a steep and narrow trail)

   _____

3. Where? (to the bottom of the canyon)

   _____

4. When? (in the early morning)

   _____

   _____

5. Why? (to ride a raft and paddle down the Colorado River)

   _____

   _____

   _____

My Final Draft

Title: The Best Vacation Ever

_____ , I went to _____

with my _____ for _____ , and it

was the best vacation I've ever had.

_____

_____

_____

_____

_____

_____

_____

_____

_____

_____

_____

<More Than 180 Words>

My Comment ☐ Good
☐ Excellent

Parent's Comment ☐ Good ☐ Excellent
Teacher's Comment ☐ Good ☐ Excellent

13

🌱 Sentence Practice

Combine the sentences using *so that*.

The conjunction *so that* shows the purpose of an action.

The robot would teach me many things. I would become a genius.
Purpose

The robot would teach me many things **so that** I would become a genius.
Conjunction

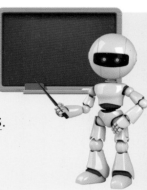

1. The homework machine would do my homework for me. I could have more time to play.

    The homework machine would do my homework for me so that I could have more time to play.

2. The flying car would take me anywhere I want to go. I could visit many famous places in the world.

    _____

    _____.

3. The cleaning robot would do the house cleaning for my mom. She would have more time to relax.

    _____

    _____.

4. The shower robot would give me a shower. I could keep myself nice and clean.

    _____

    _____.

5. The flying car would take me to school. I would always get there on time.

_____

_____ .

6. The cooking robot would cook for me. I could eat delicious food at every meal.

_____

_____ .

7. The good-friend robot would play with me. I would never be lonely.

_____

_____ .

8. The security robot would guard my house. My family could be safe all the time.

_____

_____ .

🌱 Revising Practice

Correct the underlined words. Rewrite the sentences.

1. The first thing I would ask for <u>are</u> a homework machine. (Subject-Verb Agreement)

_____ .

2. If I <u>find</u> a magic lamp and a genie granted me three wishes, it would make me feel very happy. (Tense)

_____

_____ .

3. The <u>fly</u> car would take me anywhere I want to go. (Word Form)

_____ .

4. <u>If my wishes could come true</u> it would make our lives very comfortable. (Punctuation)

_____ .

Expanding Sentences

Expand the sentences below by answering the questions using the given words.

Example: The boy would make a wish.

- **Who?** My friend Sammy would make a wish.
- **What?** My friend Sammy would make a wish for a homework machine.
- **Where?** My friend Sammy would make a wish for a homework machine in his bedroom.
- **When?** My friend Sammy would make a wish for a homework machine in his bedroom if he found a magic lamp and a genie granted him a wish.
- **Why?** My friend Sammy would make a wish for a homework machine in his bedroom if he found a magic lamp and a genie granted him a wish so that he could have more time to play.

The man would ask for a flying car and visit many famous places.

1. Who? (My favorite uncle, John,)

   _____

2. What? (would ask for a flying car with fancy wings and visit many famous places)

   _____

3. Where? (around the world)

   _____

4. When? (if he found a magic lamp and a genie granted him a wish)

   _____

   _____

5. Why? (so that he could learn about those places)

   _____

   _____

   _____

Title: **Three Wishes**

If I found a magic lamp and a genie granted me three wishes, it would make me feel _____.

<More Than 180 Words>

My Comment ☐ Good
☐ Excellent

Parent's Comment ☐ Good ☐ Excellent
Teacher's Comment ☐ Good ☐ Excellent

A Sports Star I Want to Be Like

Language Sprouts

🌱 Sentence Practice

Combine the sentences using a *that*-clause.

A *that*-clause describes a noun before it. The word *that* connects the sentence parts.

I want to be like Kim Yuna. The first reason is because she is a great figure skater.

→ The first **reason that** I want to be like Kim Yuna [is] because she is a great figure skater.

   Noun   *that*-Clause

1. I want to be like Lionel Messi. The first **reason** is because he is the best soccer player ever.

   The first reason that I want to be like Lionel Messi is because he is the best soccer player ever   .

2. I want to be like Usain Bolt. The second **reason** is because he is the fastest man alive.

   _____

   _____.

3. I want to be like Serena Williams. The last **reason** is because she is a giving person.

   _____

   _____.

4. I want to be like Kim Yuna. The **reason** is because she is a warm-hearted person.

   _____

   _____.

5. I practice a lot. The **reason** is because I want to be like Serena.

_____

_____ .

6. I work really hard. The **reason** is because I want to be the best basketball player.

_____

_____ .

7. I like Kevin Durant. The **reason** is because he is a great basketball player.

_____

_____ .

8. I want to be like Lindsey Vonn. The **reason** is because she is the best skier.

_____

_____ .

Revising Practice

Correct the underlined words. Rewrite the sentences.

1. She <u>earn</u> a lot of money from advertising. (Subject-Verb Agreement)

_____ .

2. It would be wonderful if I <u>grow</u> up to be like Yuna Kim. (Tense)

_____ .

3. She is one of the greatest <u>player</u> in the world. (Word Form)

_____ .

4. She is <u>beautiful graceful, and</u> powerful. (Punctuation)

_____ .

19

Expanding Sentences

Expand the sentences below by answering the questions using the given words.

Example: She is a figure skater, and she has won many medals.

- **Who?** Kim Yuna is a figure skater, and she has won many medals.
- **What?** Kim Yuna is one of the greatest female figure skaters, and she has won many medals.
- **Where?** Kim Yuna is one of the greatest female figure skaters in the world, and she has won many medals.
- **When?** Kim Yuna is one of the greatest female figure skaters in the world, and she has won many medals during her career.
- **How?** Kim Yuna is one of the greatest female figure skaters in the world, and she has won many medals during her career after years of hard work.

The girl donates money to charity.

1. Who? (The girl who is a famous sports star)

   _____

2. What? (donates a lot of money)

   _____

3. Where? (to charity in many poor countries)

   _____

4. When? (whenever she earns money from competitions and advertising)

   _____

   _____

5. Why? (because she has a warm and generous heart)

   _____

   _____

   _____

Title: A Sports Star I Want to Be Like

_____ is my favorite sport, and I want to be like

_____ , who is _____ .

<More Than 190 Words>

My Comment	☐ Good		
	☐ Excellent		

Parent's Comment	☐ Good	☐ Excellent
Teacher's Comment	☐ Good	☐ Excellent

6 Places I Want to Visit

Language Sprouts

🌱 Sentence Practice

Combine the sentences using a *which*-clause.

A *which*-clause describes the noun before it, and *which* connects the sentence parts.
(Put a comma [,] before a *which-clause*.)

I want to visit **Buckingham Palace**. **It** is the home of the English royal family.

→ I want to visit **Buckingham Palace, which** is the home of the English royal family.

Noun   *which*-Clause

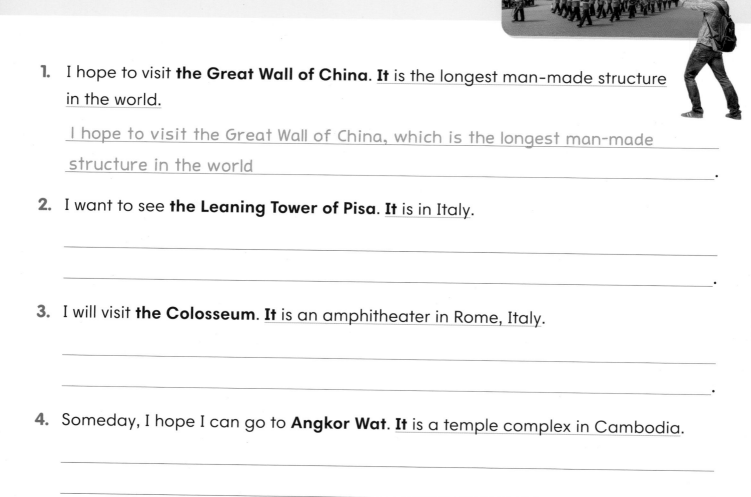

1. I hope to visit **the Great Wall of China**. **It** is the longest man-made structure in the world.

   I hope to visit the Great Wall of China, which is the longest man-made structure in the world.

2. I want to see **the Leaning Tower of Pisa**. **It** is in Italy.

   _____

   _____.

3. I will visit **the Colosseum**. **It** is an amphitheater in Rome, Italy.

   _____

   _____.

4. Someday, I hope I can go to **Angkor Wat**. **It** is a temple complex in Cambodia.

   _____

   _____.

5. I want to visit **the Eiffel Tower**. <u>It was built in Paris in the 1800s.</u>

_____

_____.

6. I am fascinated by **Niagara Falls**. <u>It is the second largest waterfall in the world.</u>

_____

_____.

7. I hope to visit **Machu Picchu**. <u>It was a city of the Inca Empire.</u>

_____

_____.

8. I want to go to **the Forbidden City**. <u>It is the largest ancient palace in the world.</u>

_____

_____.

🌱 Revising Practice

Correct the underlined words. Rewrite the sentences.

1. Another place I want to go to <u>are</u> Egypt. (Subject-Verb Agreement)

_____.

2. It is the <u>long</u> river in the world. (Word Form)

_____.

3. It would be very <u>excited</u> to walk along the top of the wall. (Word Form)

_____.

4. I hope to <u>going</u> to New York someday. (Word Form)

_____.

Expanding Sentences

Expand the sentences below by answering the questions using the given words.

Example: The girl wants to see the Great Sphinx of Giza.

- **Who?**   My cousin Sue wants to see the Great Sphinx of Giza.
- **What?**   My cousin Sue wants to see the mysterious Great Sphinx of Giza.
- **Where?**   My cousin Sue wants to see the mysterious Great Sphinx of Giza in Egypt.
- **When?**   My cousin Sue wants to see the mysterious Great Sphinx of Giza in Egypt during her next summer vacation.
- **Why?**   My cousin Sue wants to see the mysterious Great Sphinx of Giza in Egypt during her next summer vacation because it is something she has always dreamed of.

The girl wants to see the Tower of Pisa.

1. Who? (My friend Jessie, who is an architect,)

   _____

2. What? (wants to see the leaning Tower of Pisa)

   _____

3. Where? (in Italy)

   _____

4. When? (after she graduates from high school)

   _____

5. Why? (because she wants to study the architecture of the tower)

   _____

   _____

My Final Draft

Title: Places I Want to Visit

There are many _____ places in the world that
I want to see, and someday _____ .

_____

_____

_____

_____

_____

_____

_____

_____

_____

_____

_____

_____

_____

_____

<More Than 190 Words>

My Comment ☐ Good ☐ Excellent

Parent's Comment ☐ Good ☐ Excellent
Teacher's Comment ☐ Good ☐ Excellent

25

A Strange/Funny Happening

🌱 Sentence Practice

Combine the sentences using the conjunction *when*.

The conjunction *when* connects sentences, and a *when*-clause tells the time something happens.

Jimmy woke up **when** Mrs. Smith opened the door.
            Conjunction

= **When** Mrs. Smith opened the door, Jimmy woke up.

(A *when*-clause can come at the beginning of the sentence.)

1. She realized it was Jimmy. She looked through the peephole on the door.

   She realized it was Jimmy when she looked through the peephole on the door.

2. She realized she was late. She heard the bell ring.

   _____

   when _____.

3. Mrs. Smith heard a loud noise. She was watching TV.

   _____

   when _____.

4. Everyone started laughing. She walked into the classroom.

   _____

   when _____.

5. An embarrassing thing happened to Mike. He woke up one Sunday morning.

   _____

   when _____.

6. He was passing the cemetery. He saw a green light rising from a grave.

When _____

_____ .

7. She saw a shining light in the forest. She thought it was a ghost.

When _____

_____ .

8. The incident happened. John was working at his office.

When _____

_____ .

🌱 Revising Practice

Correct the underlined words. Rewrite the sentences.

1. She thought it <u>is</u> a burglar. (Tense)

_____ .

2. Jimmy was really embarrassed and just <u>wants</u> to disappear somewhere. (Tense)

_____ .

3. An <u>embarrassed</u> thing happened to Melanie. (Word Form)

_____ .

4. He knocked <u>loud</u> on the front door. (Word Form)

_____ .

Expanding Sentences

Expand the sentences below by answering the questions using the given words.

> **Example:** Jimmy had a strange thing happen to him.
>
> - **Who?** Jimmy, a boy from down the street, had a strange thing happen to him.
> - **When?** Jimmy, a boy from down the street, had a strange thing happen to him last Sunday night.
> - **What?** Jimmy, a boy from down the street, had a strange thing happen to him last Sunday night when he went to bed in his house and woke up in another place.
> - **Where?** Jimmy, a boy from down the street, had a strange thing happen to him last Sunday night when he went to bed in his house and woke up at the front door of his neighbor's house.
> - **Why?** Jimmy, a boy from down the street, had a strange thing happen to him last Sunday night when he went to bed in his house and woke up at the front door of his neighbor's house because he had been sleepwalking.

My sister had a funny thing happen to her.

1. Who? (My younger sister)

    _____

2. What? (had a funny thing happen to her when she stepped in wet cement)

    _____

3. Where? (on a new sidewalk in our neighborhood)

    _____

4. When? (on her way to school one morning last week)

    _____

    _____

5. Why? (she was reading a book and wasn't paying attention to where she was going)

    _____

    _____

My Final Draft

Title: A Strange/Funny Happening

A very _____ thing happened to

_____ when _____

_____

_____

_____

_____

_____

_____

_____

_____

_____

_____

_____

_____

<More Than 200 Words>

My Comment ☐ Good ☐ Excellent

Parent's Comment ☐ Good ☐ Excellent
Teacher's Comment ☐ Good ☐ Excellent

29

🌱 Sentence Practice

Change the underlined verb form and rewrite the sentences.

To + verb and verb-*ing* can be a subject, an object, or a complement.

I want **to be** a pilot.
Object

I **enjoy using my imagination**.
Object

To become a pilot is not easy.
Subject

Becoming a pilot is not easy.
Subject

It is not easy **to become** a pilot. (the more common form)

1. I want <u>be</u> an inventor. (to)

   I want to be an inventor   .

2. I love <u>entertain</u> people. (-ing)

   _____ .

3. John wants <u>become</u> a scientist. (to)

   _____ .

4. Inventors enjoy <u>make</u> things that improve our lives. (-ing)

   _____ .

5. I hope <u>help</u> people someday. (to)

   _____ .

6. Betty loves <u>use</u> her imagination. (-ing)

   _____ .

7. <u>Become</u> a doctor would be difficult. (-ing)

_____.

8. <u>Become</u> an astronaut would be exciting and fun. (-ing)

_____.

9. It would be exciting <u>control</u> a huge airplane in the air. (to)

_____.

10. It would be fun <u>work</u> on new science projects. (to)

_____.

Revising Practice

Correct the underlined words. Rewrite the sentences.

1. Many pilots <u>makes</u> a lot of money. (Subject-Verb Agreement)

_____.

2. Pilots are well paid <u>so</u> they receive special training for a long time. (Word Choice)

_____.

3. I will study hard and <u>doing</u> my best to achieve my goal. (Word Form)

_____.

4. <u>When I grow up</u> I want to be a book designer. (Punctuation)

_____.

Expanding Sentences

Expand the sentences below by answering the questions using the given words.

Example: David wants to be a pilot.

- **Who?** My brother David wants to be a pilot.
- **What?** My brother David wants to be an airline pilot.
- **Where?** My brother David wants to be an airline pilot for All World Airlines.
- **When?** My brother David wants to be an airline pilot for All World Airlines after he graduates from university.
- **Why?** My brother David wants to be an airline pilot for All World Airlines after he graduates from university because he can make a lot of money and see the world.

Pilots wear uniforms and hats.

1. Who? (Airline pilots)

   _____

2. What? (wear dark uniforms with stripes on the sleeves)

   _____

3. Where? (at work)

   _____

4. When? (when they fly an airplane)

   _____

   _____

5. Why? (so that passengers on the plane will know that they are real pilots)

   _____

   _____

   _____

Title: The Best Job in the World

When I grow up, I want to be _____ because
I think it is the best job in the world.

_____

_____

_____

_____

_____

_____

_____

_____

_____

_____

_____

_____

_____

<More Than 200 Words>

My Comment ☐ Good
☐ Excellent

Parent's Comment ☐ Good ☐ Excellent
Teacher's Comment ☐ Good ☐ Excellent